ENERGY THAT IS ALL AROUND

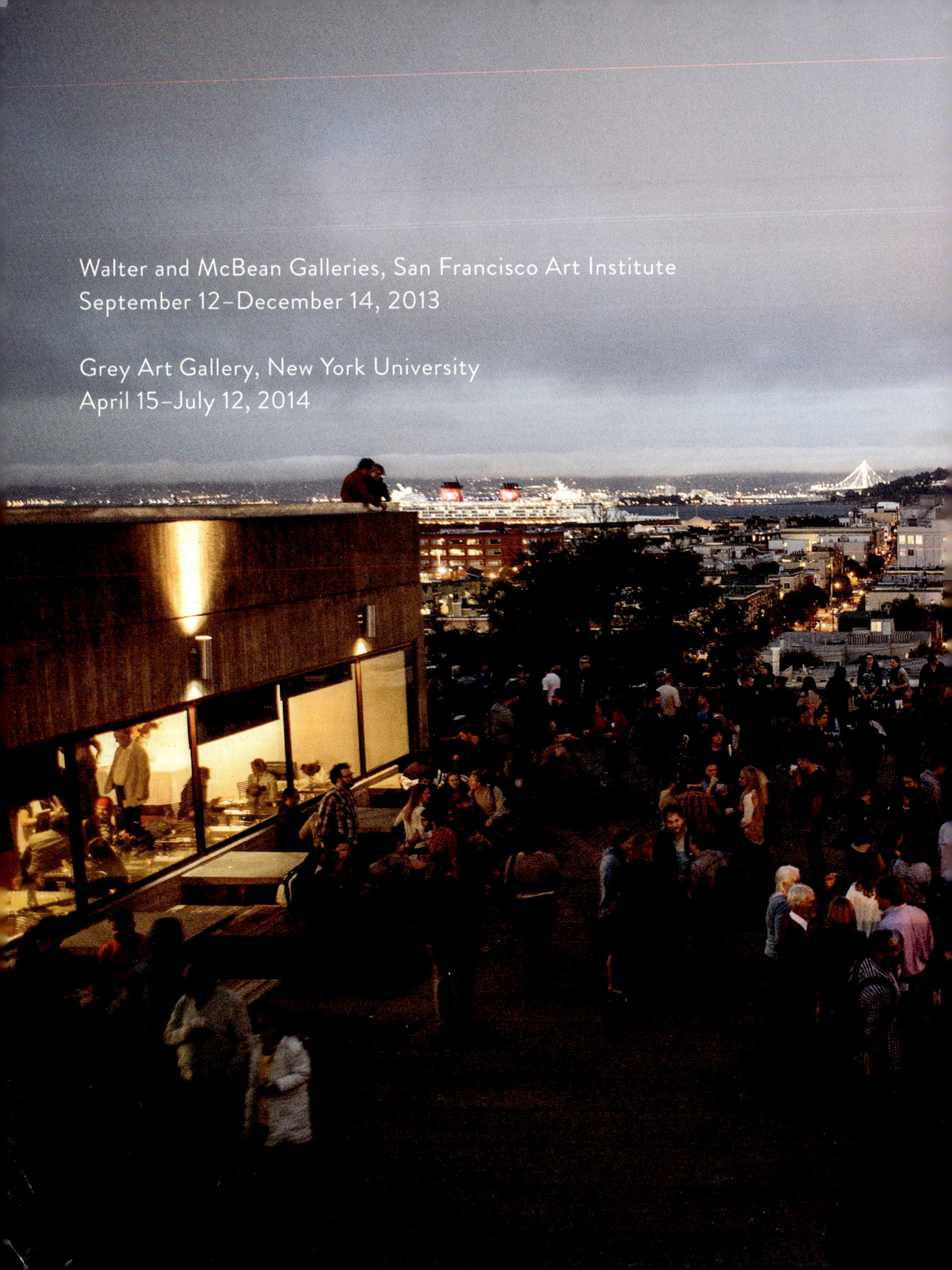

Walter and McBean Galleries, San Francisco Art Institute
September 12–December 14, 2013

Grey Art Gallery, New York University
April 15–July 12, 2014

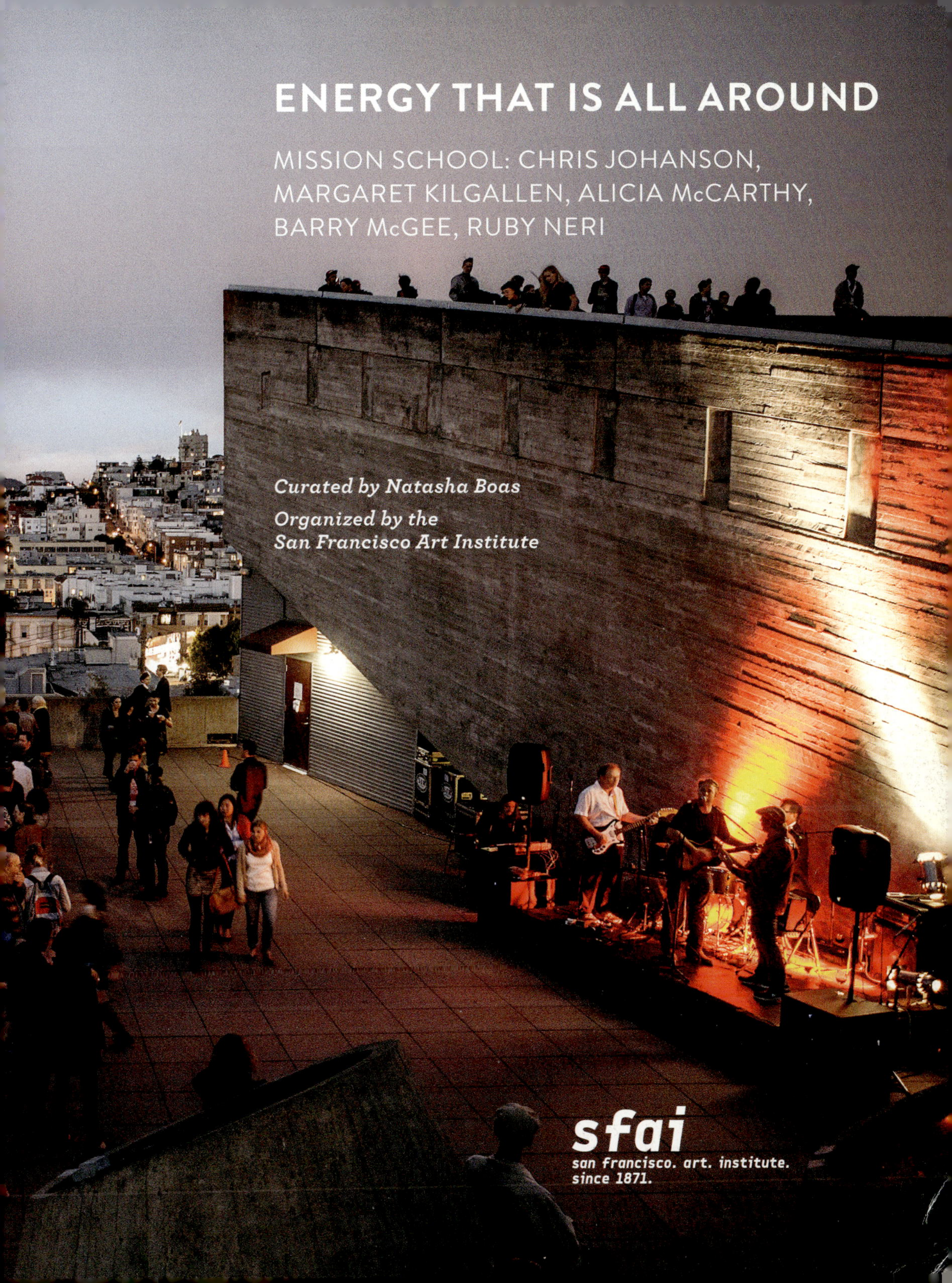

ENERGY THAT IS ALL AROUND

MISSION SCHOOL: CHRIS JOHANSON, MARGARET KILGALLEN, ALICIA McCARTHY, BARRY McGEE, RUBY NERI

Curated by Natasha Boas

Organized by the San Francisco Art Institute

sfai
san francisco. art. institute.
since 1871.

Photo on page 2: Virgil Shaw and band perform at the opening reception for ENERGY THAT IS ALL AROUND *at the San Francisco Art Institute.*

Page 117 constitutes a continuation of the copyright page.

Library of Congress Cataloging-in-Publication Data available.
Trade edition ISBN 978-1-4521-4218-0
SFAI edition ISBN 978-0-615-98873-3

Manufactured in Canada.

Design by Pamela Geismar.

10 9 8 7 6 5 4 3 2 1

Chronicle Books LLC
680 Second Street
San Francisco, CA 94107

www.chroniclebooks.com

CONTENTS

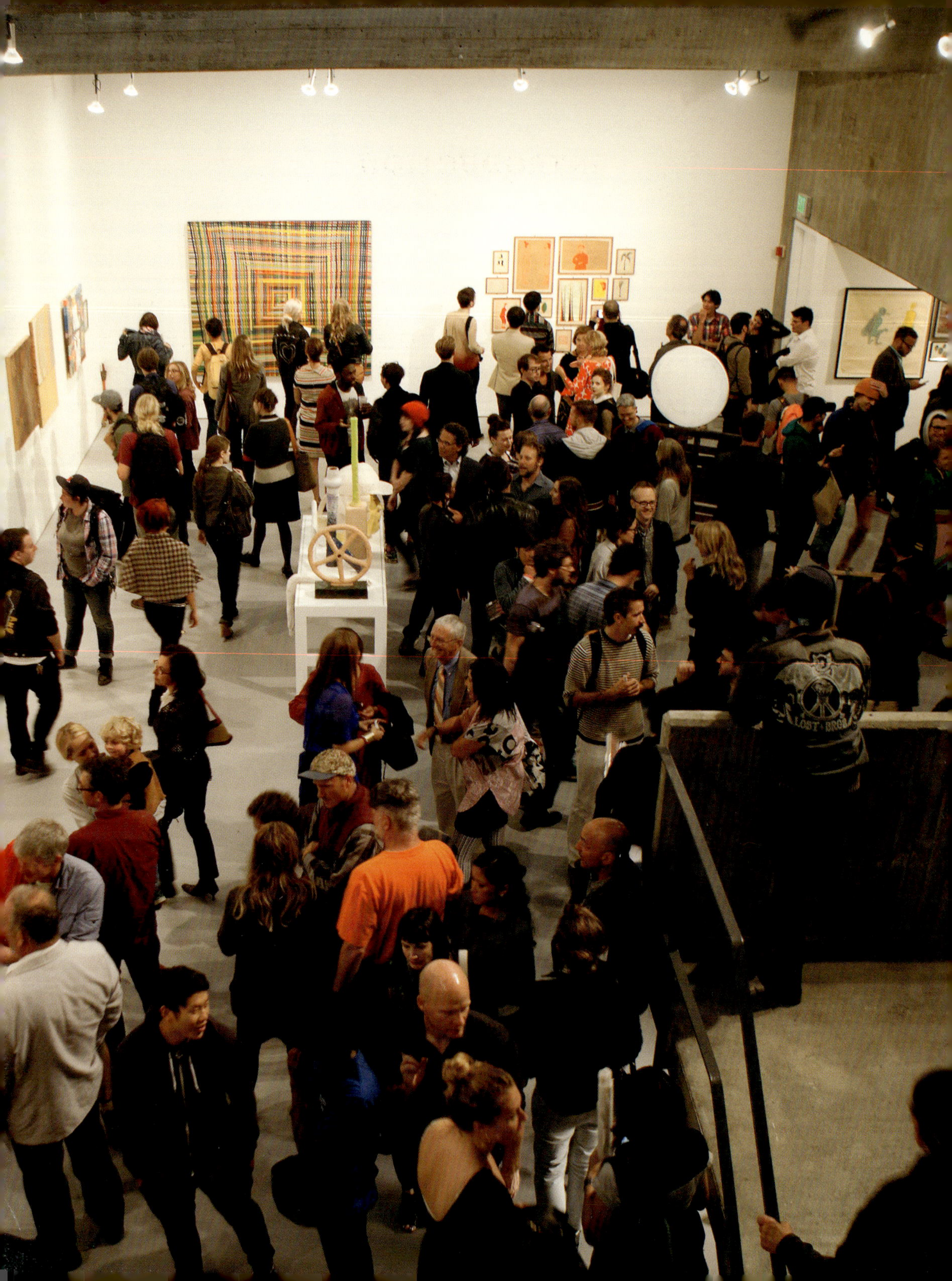

INTRODUCTION

ENERGY THAT IS ALL AROUND was the first exhibition mounted after I joined the San Francisco Art Institute—it was a raffish and spirited introduction to the idiosyncrasies and human legacy of the Institute. The artists of the Mission School have been mythologized nationally and internationally in the last decade, and this exhibition served both to demythologize these five individual artists and to relieve the fatigue from exposure that some local audiences experienced. Through this show, we were able to experience something new, soulful, personal, and immediate in their work.

I have long considered art school to be the best place on earth—it's a place where artists must work out singular paths through the roiling dynamic of a nascent and temporary community. In art school, as in life, taste is a battleground. Yet through this frisson, from time to time, a school of artists emerges that shifts the terrain for all of us. Through their various formal and informal affiliations with the San Francisco Art Institute, Chris, Margaret, Barry, Alicia, and Ruby changed the language of this institution. They have come to reflect the highest achievement of an art school, which is to cultivate artists whose work adds new strains to contemporary art, and perhaps more importantly, who care about each other enough to add life to a community of artists.

I would like to acknowledge the SFAI staff and supporters whose efforts made this exhibition possible. I would particularly like to thank Katie Hood Morgan, our Assistant Curator and Exhibitions Manager, who worked tirelessly on this exhibition. Additionally, many SFAI staff provided essential support: SFAI President Charles Desmarais, Janette Andrawes, Cynthia Colebrook, Elizabeth O'Brien, Espi Sanjana, Rachel Schreiber, Jeff Gunderson, Trevor Hacker, Katrina Herman, Heather Hickman Holland, Kent Long, Andrew McClintock, Marci Scott, John Seden, Anne Shulock, Polly Springhorn, and, of course, others. Gratitude is due to the SFAI Public Programs staff: Barbara Garber, Emily Shallman, JD Beltran, and Glen Helfand.

Lynn Gumpert and the entire staff at the Grey Art Gallery at New York University provided early support and encouragement to this exhibition, and we are honored that the exhibition will find a second home at the Grey Art Gallery.

I would also like to extend a special thanks to the artists, their galleries, lenders, and the SFAI Board of Trustees who supported this exhibition.

I would like to especially recognize Natasha Boas, who brought this exhibition to SFAI out of love for these artists and their work, and whose energy is also a force to be reckoned with. Natasha, along with Assistant Curator Nicole Crescenzi, summoned an exhibition that was critically necessary and contextually obvious, yet curiously untapped. We are very proud to have hosted this thoughtful, incisive, and gloriously unhinged exhibition.

HESSE McGRAW
VICE PRESIDENT FOR EXHIBITIONS AND PUBLIC PROGRAMS
SAN FRANCISCO ART INSTITUTE

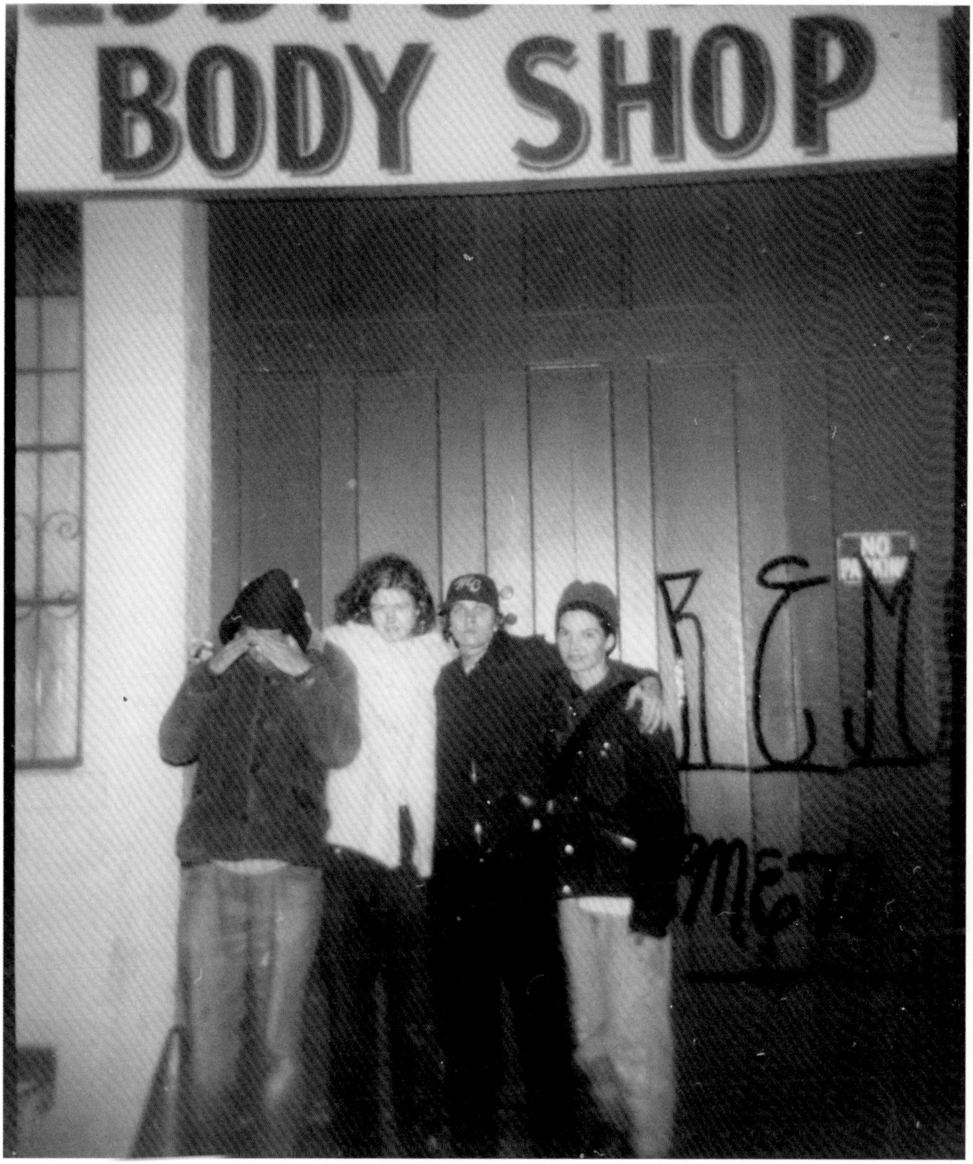

Barry McGee, Margaret Kilgallen, Alicia McCarthy, and Ruby Neri, 1994
Silver gelatin print

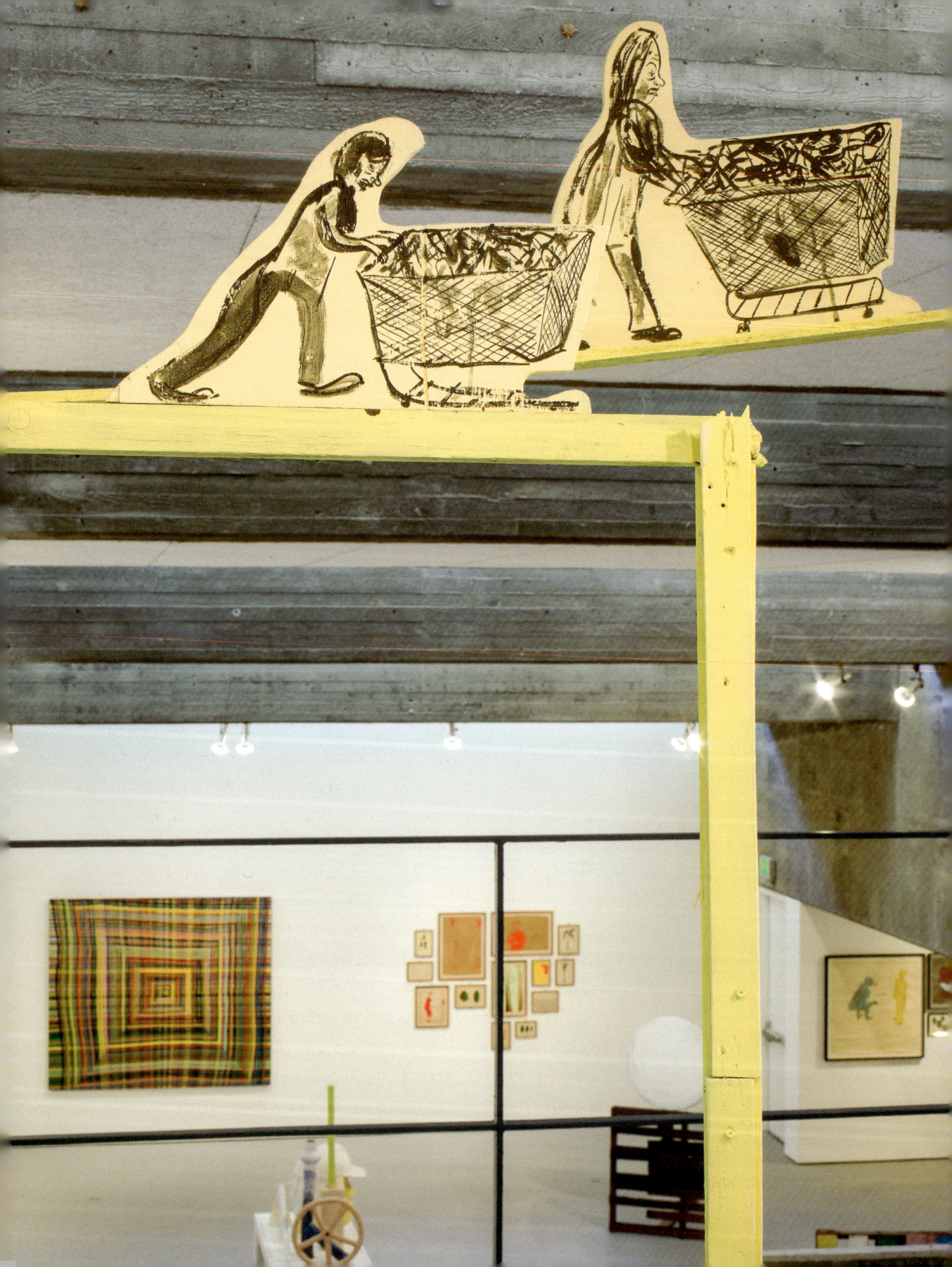

NOSTALGIA IS NO LONGER WHAT IT USED TO BE

The Making of *ENERGY THAT IS ALL AROUND*

BY NATASHA BOAS, Ph.D

"What is aura? A peculiar web of space and time: the unique manifestation of a distance, however near it may be."

WALTER BENJAMIN, "A SHORT HISTORY OF PHOTOGRAPHY//1931"

AS A SAN FRANCISCO NATIVE and a curator at the San Francisco Museum of Craft and Folk Art (MOCFA) from 2009 to 2013, I was uniquely poised to consider the intersection of craft and folk art with contemporary art and technology. I discovered that so many contemporary artists had an altogether new relationship to craft and outsider art, through which they interrogated both material and social histories. As they mined the productive tension between social networking and the global art market and slow and local community movements, their engagement with craft and folk art enabled a radicalizing of media that suggested a reaction to the present need to detechnologize, to individualize, and to galvanize disrupted communities. Trends in exhibition and art making reflect the increasing presence of social practice in art schools with the emphasis on community and collaborations, the cult of "authenticity," the aesthetic of nostalgia, the repurposing of materials, the deep romance of the handmade and a

CHRIS JOHANSON
THE SURVIVALISTS
(installation view), 1999

pretechnological culture—all of which celebrate an intentionally démodé approach to material culture through a contemporary digitized perspective.

It was through this very optic and a focus on the tension that arises from the direct cohabitation of Internet technology, new media, and the handmade with its resulting surplus of *the nostalgic* that I started to look back at those artists whom I had witnessed come of age in the early '90s while I was a curator at Yerba Buena Center for the Arts. These artists came up in art school in the pre-Internet age and started their art careers on the very cusp of the digital age at the beginning of a new optimistic decade, defined by Clinton's election, Mandela's release from prison, and an energized rebellion against the material and Republican-dominated '80s.

The city that formed Chris Johanson, Margaret Kilgallen, Alicia McCarthy, Barry McGee, and Ruby Neri had been hit hard by the AIDS epidemic. It would shortly, with its proximity to Silicon Valley, experience a culture-shattering dot-com technology boom/bust in the mid to late '90s (California's second gold rush) and was populated by increasing homelessness, drugs, and crime.

The artists lived and worked in the Mission District, a still predominantly ungentrified Latino neighborhood south of Market with low rents, devalued properties, and abandoned spaces. They were forced to assimilate the rapid and culture-shocking rise of Silicon Valley's profound mono-industrial impact on the Bay Area and beyond, where the web went from being in the backyard of culture to a mainstream playground, from Palo Alto, through the streets of SF, to the globe. Resisting the voracious appetite of the all-encompassing technological machine, these artists produced uncompromising work that still resonates strongly today in the hyper-Internet world.

In the early to mid '90s, it was still a place of fringe-dwellers and dreamers with its legendary bohemian-inflected vibe

MARGARET KILGALLEN
UNTITLED, *ca. 2000*

embracing artists, writers, surfers, skaters, musicians, and alternative lifestyles, all largely due to still-affordable rent, utopian mythologies, and active "disobedient" subcultures. The *ENERGY THAT IS ALL AROUND* artists were already delivering work that was hitting contemporary frequencies and radicalized variants in folk, zines, community, street art, and graffiti production, saturating the art scene with actively visible social conscience. Their image-generating community was responding acidly and rabidly to the social and aesthetic values associated with '80s' consumer culture, corporate hegemony, and the rising stakes of the new "super highway." These postpunk Mission School artists would soon become international icons for new generations of makers and art students with their raw, immediate, and gritty street and studio practices and their spontaneous exhibition-making impulses.

It's a well-known fact that each of the featured five artists were graffiti taggers—part of a group of San Francisco Art Institute undergrads who started marking the streets and painting "lowbrow," cartoonish, and often very humorous murals as well as various signs and symbols that were understood only by friends and initiates. The group acquired the name "Mission School" retroactively, when critic Glen Helfand coined the term in a 2002 article in an attempt to understand the fame and notoriety that McGee, Johanson, and Kilgallen in particular were experiencing on a global level with their energetic, nervy, explosive exhibitions in New York and Tokyo and inclusions in the Venice and Whitney Biennials. For Helfand, Sixteenth Street and Mission had "become the locus of a yet to be labeled brand of art that's become one of San Francisco's most notable exports," and his label stuck.[1] As his article's subtitle deftly summarized, "San Francisco's street artists had somehow managed to deliver their neighborhood to the art world."[2] Not even a decade later, in 2010, on the occasion of its seventy-fifth anniversary, the San Francisco Museum of Modern Art canonized these high-octane formerly underground painters by stating in no unequivocal terms that the Mission School was the "most significant art movement to emerge out of San Francisco in the late twentieth century."

Throughout the Mission District and the city in the early to mid '90s, the legendary bad girl Ruby Neri, tag name REM, short for "Reminisce," illicitly painted monochromatic, anatomically impeccable horses. Alicia McCarthy, with her studio based at Epicenter—a queer punk underground collective—was "Fancy" and "Probe" written out in antique cursive script in pencil and paint. "Meta," Kilgallen, reworked hobo art and imagery and offered her own folksy font interpretation of conventional sign making and advertising. McGee, "Twist," turned out his Philip Gustonian angst-ridden urban characters. Johanson, with his black Sharpie, created infamously angry stick figures accompanied by scrawled, outlandishly poetic social provocations that populated every available SF wall and civic outlet. Chris Johanson's *Life Is Shit* triptych that is included in the show is a strong example of the kind of sped-up, angsty, ironic, rebellious representation one could see on mailboxes and storefronts in the early '90s. These artists and their wider community painted Clarion Alley mural projects, the Redstone Building, and signage for the LAB; showed at Jack Hanley Gallery, New Langton Arts, the Luggage Store; filled Adobe Books' backroom with painting; and activated so many of the alternative art spaces in the city with their music, presence, and an expanded group of like-minded friends and artists.

Four of these artists, minus Margaret Kilgallen—who died in 2001—continue to collaborate today, long after having established themselves in institutions, galleries, and private collections. Although the exhibition may take as its premise and proposition the styles and close formal and affective affinities that these artists shared then and continue to share now—at times the works in the show are rendered indistinguishable through curatorial selection and exhibition design—it also highlights the strong individual career

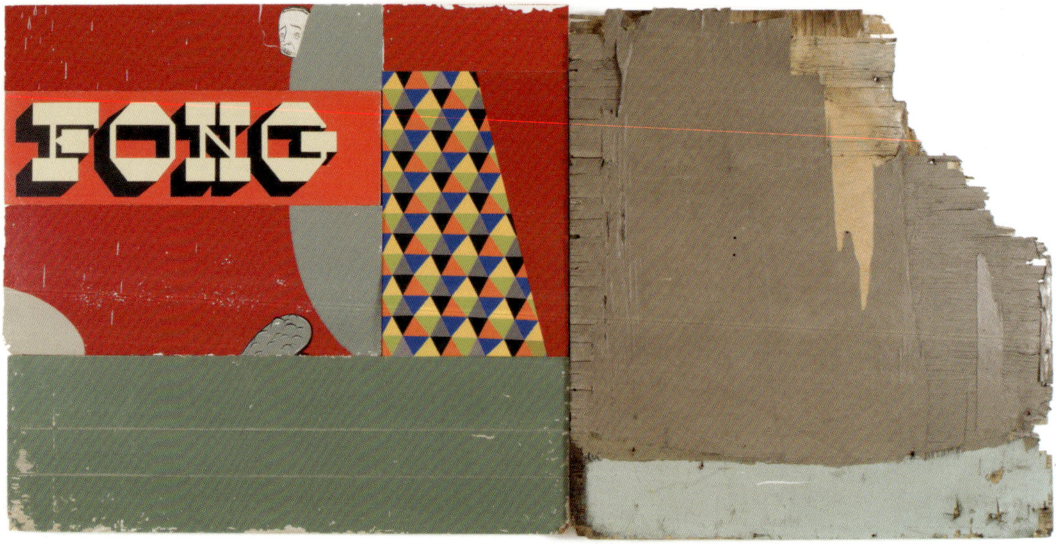

arcs and trajectories of unique practitioners. The multivalent approach to the exhibition and its many narrative visual strains and references attempt to reflect both the ambivalence that artists have to being identified with a particular movement as well as their enthusiasm for the very movement they are aligned with and helped create.

Barry McGee's commissioned work for this exhibition, *Untitled*, 1990–2013, acts as a conceptual lynchpin for the show. It is composed of a large partially painted and damaged panel retrieved from a storefront in the Mission in the early '90s, built up with many elements taken from his work and the streets over the last two decades, including another moniker, "Fong," a scattering of his cartoon figurative teases, and a recent abstract geometric painting—a literal "re-collection" of elements that span McGee's life as a graffiti artist to his work now as a gallery artist. In many ways this painting tells a story of the arc and continuum of the so-called Mission School—not only in its materiality but also in its narrative panel elements. *Untitled*, 1990–2013, is a visual time capsule for *ENERGY THAT IS ALL AROUND*.

left
BARRY McGEE
UNTITLED, *1990–2013*

right
BARRY McGEE
UNTITLED *(installation view), ca. 1998*

Over the years Barry McGee has emerged as the poster child for the group and may be its most recognizable member in the global art world. In 2012, the Berkeley Art Museum organized his midcareer survey show constructed around the idea of "bringing the street into the museum."[3] Although the McGee survey was infused with a heavy disenfranchised street-level tenor, paradoxically, it made even more evident the fact that McGee moved seamlessly from the night streets of the 1990s' Mission district into institutional spaces and commercial galleries over the last decades, developing an important and thriving gallery presence without wandering far from his San Francisco graffiti roots. Like his New York counterparts Jean-Michel Basquiat and Keith Haring, Barry McGee is credited as having elevated graffiti to an art form, garnering critical esteem in the global art world and opening institutionally sanctioned doors. As Ruby Neri points out, "Barry was instrumental in bringing what he did on the street into the gallery. He worked at a printing shop in the early '90s and used lots of cast-off material in his work. He also found objects from the street and combines these objects with his street sensibilities into an installation environment in a gallery setting. I think of this as a way of working when I think of what people call the 'Mission School.'"[4]

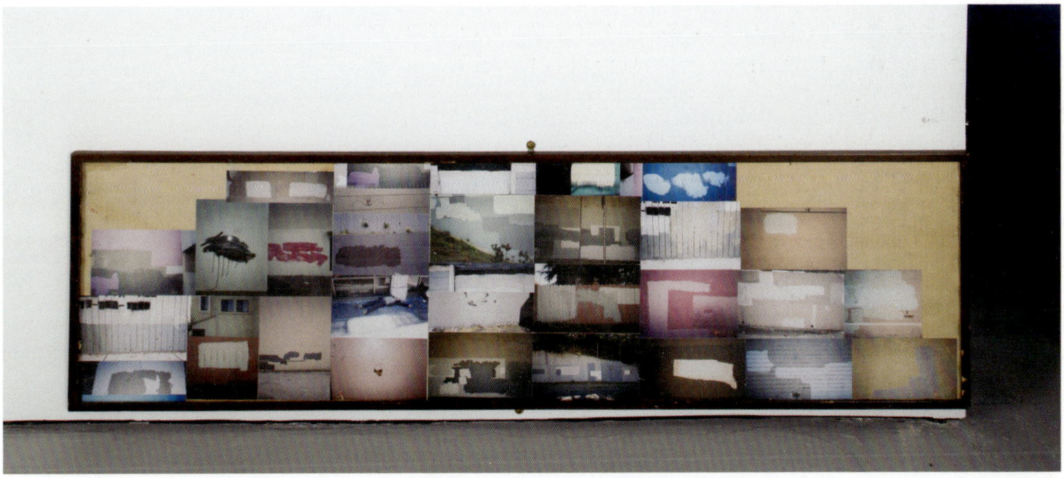

Over the decades, Johanson, Kilgallen, McCarthy, McGee, and Neri have all been afforded popular museum and commercial gallery shows as part of a larger group such as *Beautiful Losers*; Bay Area Now exhibitions at Yerba Buena Center for the Arts; slap-up casual postgraffiti installations at RARE Gallery in New York; Deitch Projects exhibitions; and, most recently, *Art in the Streets* at MOCA, Los Angeles. These shows and the 2008 film *Beautiful Losers* by Aaron Rose offered up a strong argument for a subversive group ethos of artists sharing something youthful, ephemeral, and rebellious in content and context of the street. But to this day, there had yet to be an exhibition that attempted to probe the reality or the myth of the so-called Mission School of the early '90s. Did old friends Chris Johanson, Alicia McCarthy, Barry McGee, Ruby Neri, and the late Margaret Kilgallen, with their shared formal and stylistic strategies in color, surface, and paint, constitute a "school"? Could we trace figurative and abstract foundations to the artists' earliest works? What, in fact, was this Mission School? What if we were to move from a previous desire to celebrate an indie naïvety and youthful rebelliousness (as was done in past shows) to looking at the formal intelligence and nuanced political positions this work represented at midcareer? What if we considered the visual politics of the works and not just those posed by tactical illegal graffiti art? Through the searching of references and early works, including school notebooks, photographs, sketches, pre-commercialized paintings, and ephemera, could we shift the primary conversation from the street to the studio?

A SCHOOL WITHIN A SCHOOL WITHIN A SCHOOL

Although San Francisco and the Mission District may have acted as muse to these artists, it is a school—the San Francisco Art Institute (SFAI)—that reveals itself as the creative platform and breeding ground. As Alicia McCarthy told me during our interview for a Mission School oral history, "I think the Mission School is a name that came from random parts that culminated in a time and place. This was Bay Area–wide and included many artists. We were very tied in to a Bay Area art history of the '40s onward like the Bay Area Figurative Movement and the Beats. We were all connected to the San Francisco Art Institute in some way."[5] Barry McGee, Ruby Neri, and Alicia McCarthy all attended SFAI as undergraduates (Ruby and Alicia shared Studio 18 and were both in the painting program, graduating in 1994, while McGee was in the printmaking program, graduating in 1991). Margaret Kilgallen, who was never actually enrolled in the school (she received her BFA in printmaking from Colorado College in 1989 and MFA from Stanford in 2001) often visited the library and campus and took non-credit courses. Chris Johanson—who had a more tenuous relationship to SFAI, not having graduated from any art school and positioning himself as the "outsider to all institutions in general"[6]—has more often than not been affiliated with a distinctly SFAI aesthetic, and exhibited his work in the early '90s with Alicia McCarthy in the Diego Rivera Gallery.[7] He was, as well, most likely drawn to SFAI's student history of punk, as this is where bands like the Mutants, the Avengers, and Romeo Void emerged. Not unlike Raymond Pettibon and his legendary graphics for Black Flag—Johanson's tense, restless, and demanding '90s' images continue an '80s' SF punk aesthetic.

In February and March of 1996, the Walter and McBean Galleries organized an alumni exhibition as part of the Institute's 125th anniversary titled *Low Cool*, which featured artists making the degraded low-value painting, drawing, and installation work that is associated with the Mission School and really underscored how SFAI played an important role in developing the aesthetic.

It is not a coincidence that Beat antiestablishment artist Joan Brown's funky sculptures—made with humble/quotidian materials such as fabric, cardboard, and fur and highlighting her underground association and anticommercial art making in the '60s—were shown alongside a Ruby Neri mural as well as several multipaneled works. Neri credits

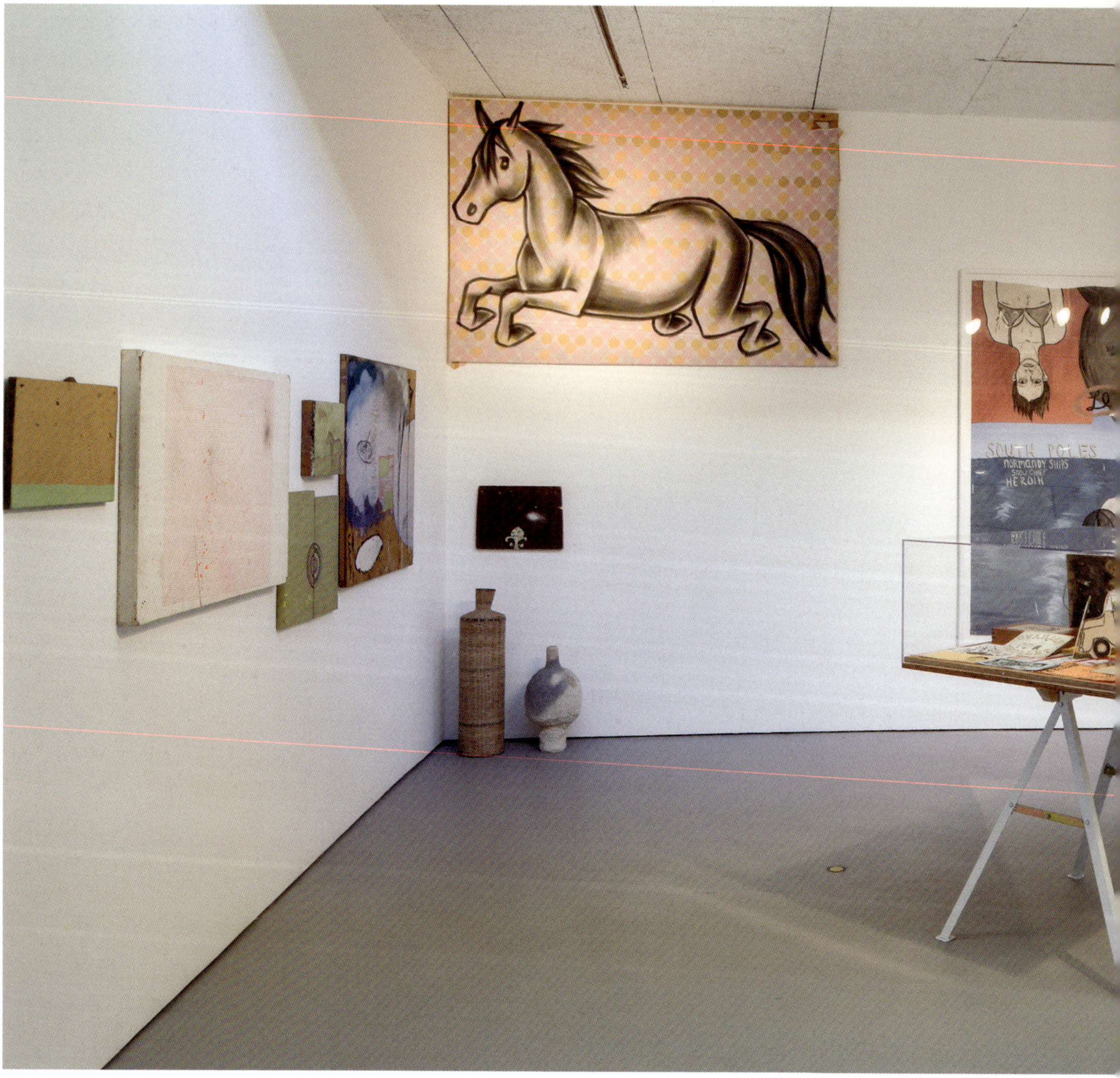
SOUTH POLES
NORMANDY SHIPS
HEROIN

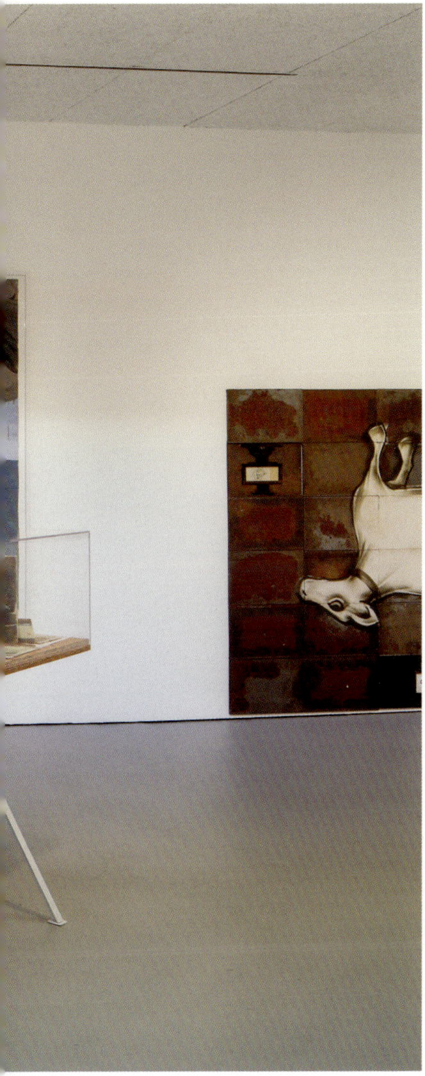

ENERGY THAT IS ALL AROUND *(installation view)*

Mike Kelley and Nicole Eisenman as influences in her perversions of pop cultural images and her provocative and outrageously sly figurative pictures. Neri's work in *ENERGY THAT IS ALL AROUND*—such as *REM Bedsheet*, a spray-painted horse on a pink-checkered sheet; her naked self-portraits; or her cat and female nude sketch from her personal diaries—speak to a liberated, libidinously charged, figurative takeover and a possible wink to (or Oedipal jab at) her illustrious painter father, Manuel Neri, also of the Bay Area Figurative Movement and professor at SFAI.

McCarthy, Neri, and Kilgallen felt strong feminist kinships in their work as well as in their close friendship. Alicia McCarthy's riffs on "weavings" in her painting index a sophisticated formal understanding of not only modernist color theories and artists such as the Bauhaus-turned-Black-Mountain-College textile- and printmaker Anni Albers but also a legacy of women-centric craft traditions. Kilgallen's caricatured postfeminist women would much rather smoke, surf, argue, and wear train-flattened coins than a proper string of pearls. Her three-dimensional Pearl piece, which showcases a signature flat hand-lettered signage and her distinct line drawing, may be one of her strongest and most elegiac pieces. It directly references her love of train hobo culture—she made line drawings on freight trains with her tag Matokie Slaughter—and her emphasis on creating independent female characters, or "heroines" as she referred to them in her *Art21* interviews on PBS. In these interviews, she talks about the importance in her art and life of making "women visible" and "the fact that maybe, maybe, somebody will learn from what I'm doing." In her brief but prolific and impressive career, Margaret Kilgallen, a dedicated typographer and printmaker, etched her own equally hard-hitting legacy and visual imprint.

McCarthy locates an important part of her painting education at SFAI, and her own unconventional use of paint in the midcentury masterpiece *The Rose* (1958–66, now in the Whitney's collection): "Strangely, Jay DeFeo's *The Rose* ended up in the McMillan Conference Room where we would sometimes have class and slide lectures next to the McBean Gallery at SFAI. It could not find a permanent museum home and it was shored up to keep it from deteriorating in a plaster mold in a temporary wall for twenty years. It was such a strong presence during my time at SFAI. You could not be a student or a painter without feeling its intensity like a haunting ghostlike presence."[8]

When the Mission School artists were on campus "learning," the Beats' lack of concern for impeccable technique, durability, or form, their DIY style, and their improvisational aesthetic still permeated SFAI. And yet it would appear that Studio 18—Barry, Ruby, and Alicia's hub—was a school unto itself—where painting students were learning from each other, rejecting mentors and art theory, and transgressing by painting on walls and neighboring houses throughout their BFA student years, soliciting strong recriminations from the administration. To this day a tag clearly made by Barry's hand persists on the ceiling in the Diego Rivera Gallery next to the historically conserved Rivera murals. Ruby Neri positions herself in a spontaneous, unmediated, romantic but sophisticated relationship to materials of all kinds without prepping, whether it was once taking spray paint to the street or now in shaping clay. In a series of letters that Michael Grady, the former dean of students at SFAI, wrote to Ruby Neri between 1991 and 1992, we discover repeated threats of dismissal and a strong confusion as to how to impose institutional sanctions on creative freedom: "Dear Ruby: Last November, I wrote a letter to you asking you to stop painting on the walls. Most recently a piece titled *Ruby's Boat*. You made no attempt to conceal the fact that you did this graffiti . . . We are not getting through to you! Doing graffiti at SFAI is unacceptable. It's destructive, aggressive, and most of all, childish."[9]

Letter dated April 8, 1992

SFAI San Francisco Art Institute
800 Chestnut Street
San Francisco, CA 94133-2299
(415) 771-7020

Alicia McCarthy
c/o SFAI Student Mailboxes

April 8, 1992.

Dear Alicia:

There has been a rash of grafitti at SFAI this semester. Discrete inquiries as to the people involved have led me to you. Although I have no concrete evidence, your name keeps coming up. It seems clear to me that you are in some way involved in these occurrences.

Grafitti is a pain in the ass for everybody at SFAI. I have been told that it's going to cost about $2000, to clean up the latest rash. That's $2000 that could have gone to equipment, scholarships, etc. At a time when the tuition is forced to go up faster than <u>anybody</u> wants it to, we cannot tolerate this kind of waste!

Why not just leave it? The short answer is that it looks like shit. If those anonymous grafitti artists delude themselves that this is art, they are mistaken. Adolescent? self-indulgent? inconsiderate? - yes. Art?... no, at least not very interesting art - just mediocre attempts at appearing "subversive".

There's another important reason why the grafitti is especially harmful. As you may be aware we are attempting to buy the GAP building. In order to obtain the zoning variances required to turn it into studio space, the neighbors (who have to look at the grafitti) will be required to give their approval. Over the years, complaints from the neighbors about grafitti have been near the top of their list. This is <u>not</u> the time to antagonize them.

My initial tendency is to dismiss this sort of thing as mere childishness. In this case, though, I can't. It has been made very clear to me by Bill Barrett and the Board that this outbreak of grafitti has really angered everyone. I'm even getting complaints about it from the other students. So, if you, or anyone else is caught doing grafitti, it is quite possible that President Barrett will exercise his exclusive right to unilaterally dismiss the party involved from SFAI. At the very least I will be forced to take judiciary action. If you are one of those who are vandalizing SFAI, stop it. If you know of others who are involved in this activity, communicate this message to them. If you wish to discuss the issue further, please meet with me in the Students Services Office. I appreciate your cooperation.

Sincerely,

Mike

Michael Grady
Dean of Students

These five artists all cite abstraction, figuration, folk art, punk music, Beat poetry, and popular and underground comics as influences in their art while contextualizing them in the very process of their work. Their collective and individual work evokes a paradox: seemingly unfinished and right off the wall but all highly considered and resolved. They move with ease between representation and abstraction, image and text, expressive and impressive modes in installations combining mural painting, public works, sculpture, drawing, and multimedia work, all with a deep fundamental interest—both owned or tacit—in the history of painting. If *ENERGY THAT IS ALL AROUND* has revealed itself as first and foremost a painting show, it is also a group exhibition-making effort by Johanson, McCarthy, McGee, and Neri to find, create, and select work that responds to the curatorial imperative of looking back and looking forward simultaneously.

The artists participated in the making of the exhibition in "Mission School style," returning with enthusiasm to their origins of experimentation and transgressions at *their* school with in situ wall paintings and sculptures as well as last-minute surprises: Ruby literally unpacking her entire archives; Chris arriving with the 12-inch cover art for *Tina, Age 30* in a thrift store frame; Alicia hauling suitcases of ephemera into the gallery; and Barry McGee's inclusion of Margaret's live succulent plants, which he pulled out of storage in their original painted pots, as well as her first two-paneled abstract painting that only those who visited her studio in the '90s would be able to identify today—souvenirs for the initiated and important indices for the uninitiated—marks of care and admiration for a talent lost in our midst. As Alicia McCarthy mentioned in her recent artist talk about the continuum in her painting practice, "I think you can't look back without looking forward, and you can't look forward without looking back."[10]

NOT FORGETTING

In a page taken from McCarthy's art history class notebook at SFAI, next to one of her recurring, meticulously perfected, endless infinity knots, she jots notes about "Historical materialism" and Walter Benjamin's notion of the "aura." It is impossible not to look at this Benjaminian shorthand without summoning the particular qualities of traditional art at the turn of the twentieth century that Benjamin observed waning in modernity, associated with the singular status of the artwork, its authenticity in the age of mass reproduction and mass spectacle. The desire for intimacy "to bring things close" that Benjamin understood as spurring the need for reproduction while stripping a work of its "aura" permeates *ENERGY THAT IS ALL AROUND* and highlights its anxious, historical fin de siècle—this time the year 2000—response to the rampant promiscuity of the now-digitized image.

The words *nostalgia* or *nostalgic* are often used in relation to the work of these five artists, with their "auratic effects" in paintings and drawings, and it would seem that we have entered an age where we have become nostalgic for nostalgia. To be sure, a grunge verve fashion is currently a global epidemic and many curators have been looking back at the early '90s. In the catalog for the 2013 exhibition at the New Museum titled *NYC 1993: Experimental Jet Set, Trash and No Star* curator Massimiliano Gioni writes, "The title draws its subtitle from the eponymous album that the New York rock band Sonic Youth recorded in 1993 and captures the complex exchange between mainstream and underground culture across disciplines, which came to define the art of the era." The twenty-year critical distance encouraged the question: Must we always wait at least twenty years to "look back" and try to historicize, and is historicizing always a nostalgic impulse?

Indeed, *nostalgia* has always been a word that signals both praise and disdain, and is a tenuous and loaded "condition." Nostalgia was first seen as a "disorder of the imagination" in the seventeenth and eighteenth centuries until

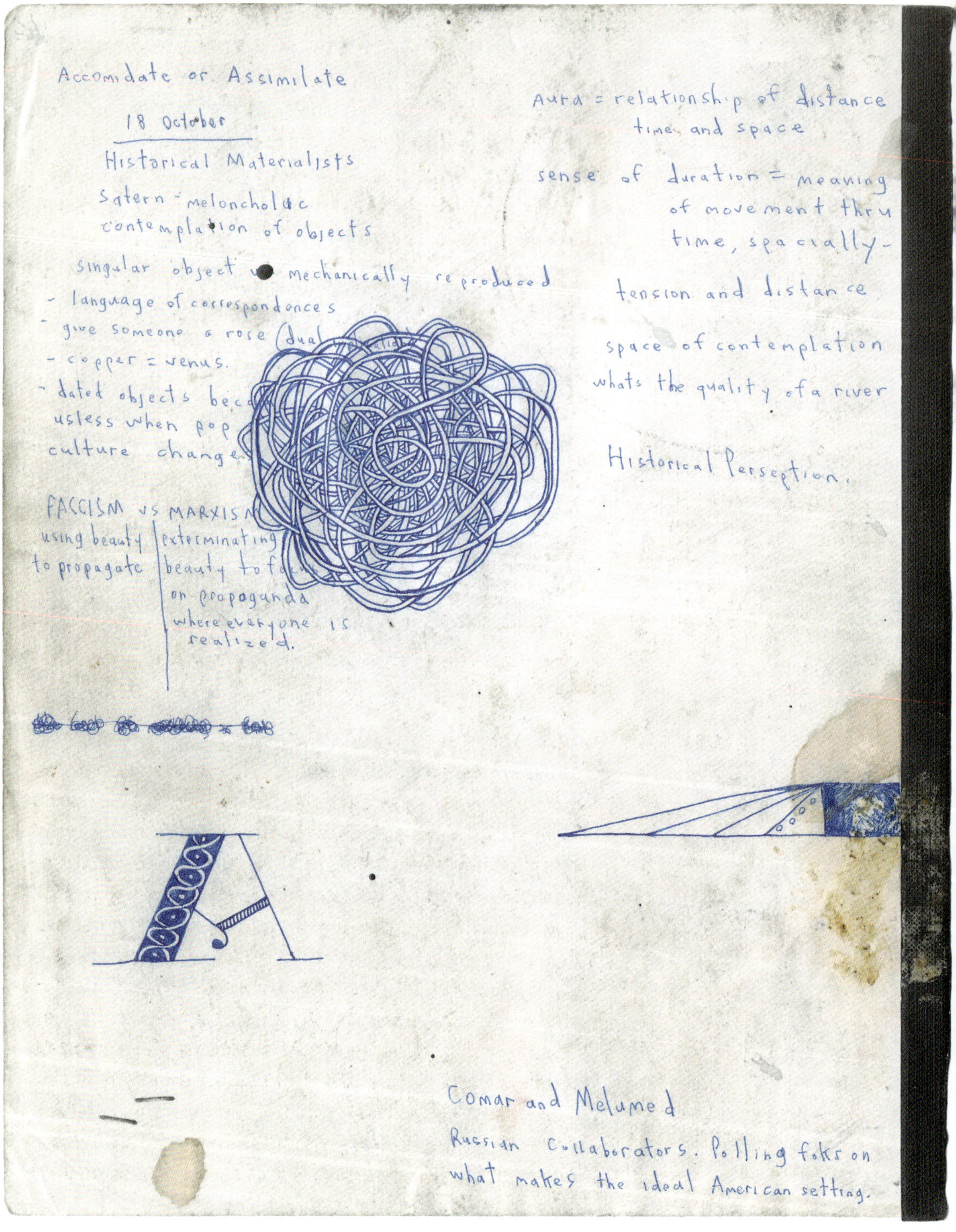

Accomidate or Assimilate

18 October

Historical Materialists

satern - meloncholdic
contemplation of objects

singular object vs mechanically reproduced

- language of correspondences
- give someone a rose (dual
- copper = venus.
- dated objects bec
usless when pop
culture change

FASCISM vs MARXISM

using beauty to propagate	exterminating beauty to focus on propaganda where everyone is realized.

Aura = relationship of distance
time and space

sense of duration = meaning
of movement thru
time, spacially -

tension and distance

space of contemplation

whats the quality of a river

Historical Perseption.

Comar and Melumed

Russian Collaborators. Polling foks on what makes the ideal American setting.

it became a physical disorder in the nineteenth century.[11] The word *nostalgia*—which comes from two Greek roots, *nostos* meaning "return home," and *algia*, "longing"—could be problematized as not only a simple "longing for a place" but also a yearning for a different time or, even more abstractly, a different "sense of time." In many ways the state of nostalgia shares two temporalities: It is more than a *souvenir* or memory; it is not only retrospective but also prospective. It is a fundamentally "now and then" problem.

Acutely aware of the nuances of time as cultural indexes, writer Rebecca Solnit writes about our current technology-induced anxiety: "I wonder sometimes if there will be a revolt against the quality of time the new technologies have brought us, as well as the corporations in charge of those technologies. Or perhaps there already has been, in a small, quiet way. The real point about the slow food movement was often missed. It wasn't food. It was about doing something from scratch, with pleasure, all the way through, in the old methodical way we used to do things. That didn't merely produce better food; it produced a better relationship to materials, processes, and labor, notably your own, before the spoon reached your mouth."[12]

Seen together as a group, the artists' work is keenly sensitive to process and labor and represents the tension between pre- and post-digitized worlds. Their use of deliberately tactile, discarded, and crafty materials upends complacency and creates dynamic, unhinged, politically charged work. Like nostalgia itself, their work points to a visceral dissatisfaction with the culture of the present. In a review of Alicia McCarthy's untitled exhibition at Jack Hanley Gallery, referring to her use of reclaimed materials, cursive fonts, and painterly strategies, Julian Myers-Szupinska suggests that nostalgia may actually be a defense against the effects and affects of technology: "These techniques are legible, in retrospect, as defensive tactics against the dot.com bomb, against its love of novelty and font-fetishism, against its slick Photoshop graphics and bubble-economy hubris."[13]

Alicia McCarthy notebook page, ca. 1996

Chris Johanson believes there is a current epidemic of amnesia in San Francisco and was adamant in bringing back his *The Survivalists* (1999) for *ENERGY THAT IS ALL AROUND*—which he has kept in his own private collection since it was first installed at the LAB in 1999. In explaining his decision to bring *The Survivalists* out of storage for this exhibition, Chris said: "San Francisco is going through another technology boom and I don't want anyone to forget the impact of the first one. This time it will have greater effects than last time. It's menacing." This protest work is a direct response to that abrupt and seismic historic moment that these five artists experienced firsthand at the turn of the millennium with its economic violence and are experiencing again with the technology sector dominating the city. Not unlike the futurist Giacomo Balla's *Bankruptcy* (1902), which painstakingly renders the narrative of foreclosure (with the summons stuffed into the neglected, graffitied ancient doors) and prompts the emergence of a new vocabulary for a new century, Johanson's *Survivalists* is an ironic clarion call to the new technology revolution and its tremulous socioeconomic impact.

Like nostalgia itself then, *ENERGY THAT IS ALL AROUND* as an exhibition shares two temporalities: 1990 and *now*. All five artists in *ENERGY THAT IS ALL AROUND* have given surplus value to what I would venture to call "edgy nostalgia" (one that does not activate sentimentality but transgresses it). If in the '80s it was irony that captured our cultural and academic attention, in the '90s nostalgia inevitably reappears as a defense mechanism in a time of accelerated rhythms of life and historical upheaval, and confuses the definitions of ironies—could nostalgia be a defense against irony or irony a defense against nostalgia? Although a large selection of '90s' work defines the show, several pieces from the 2000s and newly commissioned work for the exhibition assure that *ENERGY THAT IS ALL AROUND* is not an archive, historic capsule, or commemoration. Rather, it puts into play the very idea of nostalgia as a

MARGARET KILGALLEN
UNTITLED, *1997*

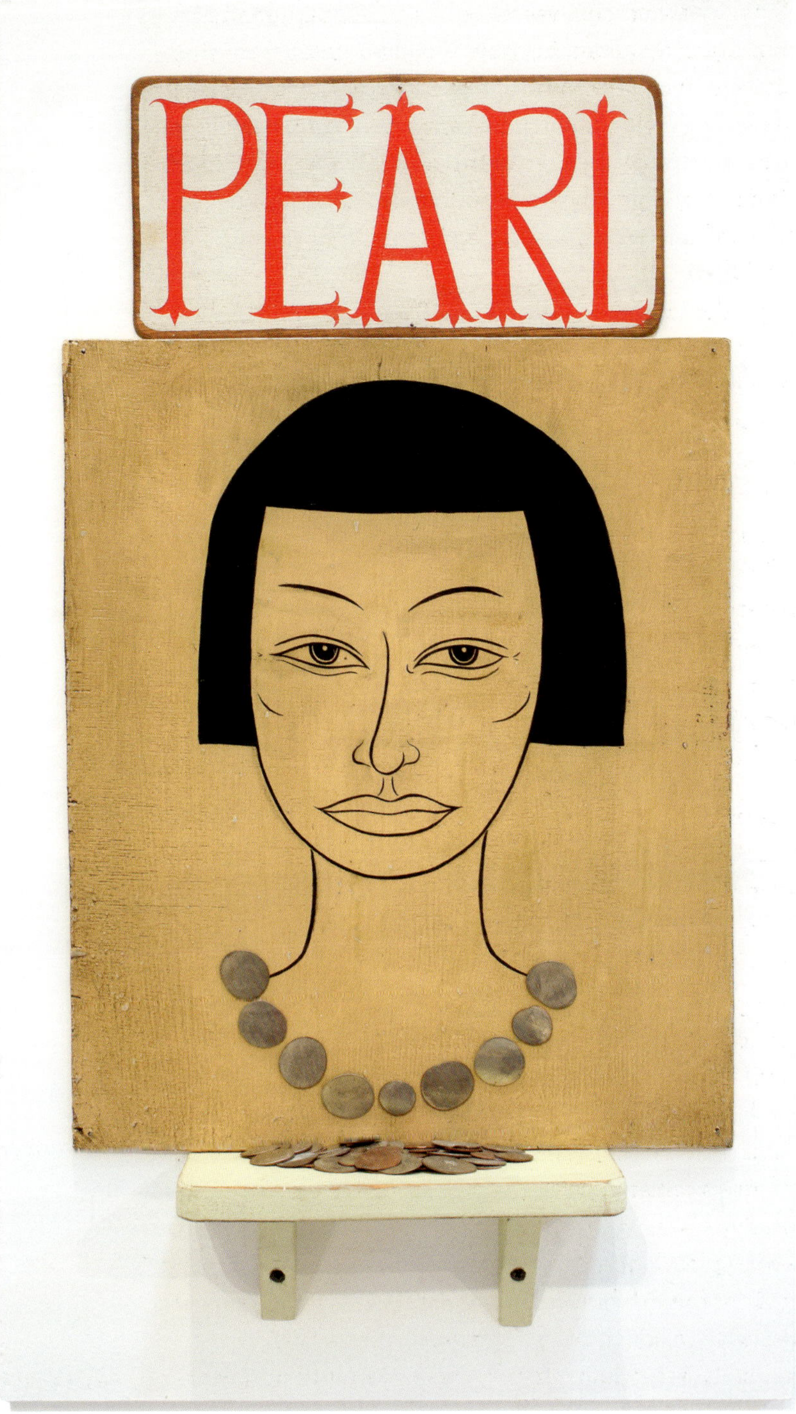
PEARL

meaningful trope for the contemporary condition. If Mission School artists—with their visual language, art practice, and lifestyles, and their particular form of collectivity, repurposing, and celebration of folk and the readymade—were already actively nostalgic in the early '90s (let's not forget Ruby Neri/"Reminisce" was reminiscing already back then), their work remains uncannily contemporary today.

ENERGY THAT IS ALL AROUND satisfied a seemingly urgent curatorial impulse to look back at an important group of artists born out of graffiti culture who continue to produce and inform today's visual language with prolific generosity and strong materiality. The original title for the show was *Folk as Fuck*, which came out of an early curatorial conversation in an effort to underline the playful, political, and rebellious roots of the artists' origins as well as their direct, unabashed celebration of folk and communal culture. Just as the main character in the Coen Brothers' film *Inside Llewyn Davis* (2013) grasps the ineffable of folk music in the noteworthy line "It's never new, it never gets old, it's a folk song," Mission School art manages to be both timeless and time-full.

Yet, it was ultimately a quote from Chris Johanson in a recent interview—"When you spend all this time doing something, you're making real energy"[14]—and words borrowed from his 2012 painting on paper that, in the end, generated the most evocative and auratic title for an exhibition, a title that produces a slip in chronological experience and an inference to something else. That something else—like nostalgia itself—is that which subsists after all and resists the historical in the present.

1 Glen Helfand, "The Mission School: San Francisco's street artists deliver their neighborhood to the art world," *San Francisco Bay Guardian*, January 3, 2002, http://www.sfbg.com/36/28/art_mission_school.html.

2 Ibid.

3 Dena Beard, "Mission School: Yes or No?" (panel discussion, San Francisco Art Institute, October 20, 2013).

4 Natasha Boas, "Was There Ever a Mission School: A Partial and Incomplete Oral History," *Barry McGee*. Berkeley: D.A.P./University of California, Berkeley Art Museum and Pacific Film Archive, 2013. Exhibition catalog, 214–15.

5 Alicia McCarthy, interview by Natasha Boas, August 2011, for *Barry McGee* by Alex Baker. Ed. Lawrence Rinder and Dena Beard. Published by D.A.P./ University of California, Berkeley Art Museum and Pacific Film Archive. Copyright © 2012 by The Regents of the University of California.

6 Chris Johanson (Visiting Artists and Scholars Lecture Series, San Francisco Art Institute, March 4, 2013).

7 *Big n' Easy*, organized by Jamie Stahley and Karla Milosevich, June 1994.

8 Alicia McCarthy, interview by Natasha Boas, August 2011, for *Barry McGee* by Alex Baker. Ed. Lawrence Rinder and Dena Beard. Published by D.A.P./ University of California, Berkeley Art Museum and Pacific Film Archive. Copyright © 2012 by The Regents of the University of California.

9 Dean of Students Michael Grady to Ruby Neri, April 8, 1992. San Francisco Art Institute Library archives, courtesy of Jeff Gunderson.

10 Alicia McCarthy (Visiting Artists and Scholars Lecture Series, San Francisco Art Institute, November 14, 2013).

11 *Oxford English Dictionary* http://www.oxforddictionaries.com/us/definition/american_english/nostalgia.

12 Rebecca Solnit, "Diary," *London Review of Books* 35, no. 16 (29 August 2013): 32–33, http://www.lrb.co.uk/v35/n16/rebecca-solnit/diary.

13 Julian Myers, "Alicia McCarthy," *Frieze* 78 (October 2003).

14 Bob Nickas, Corrina Peipon, and Julie Deamer, *Chris Johanson* (London: Phaidon, 2013), 14.

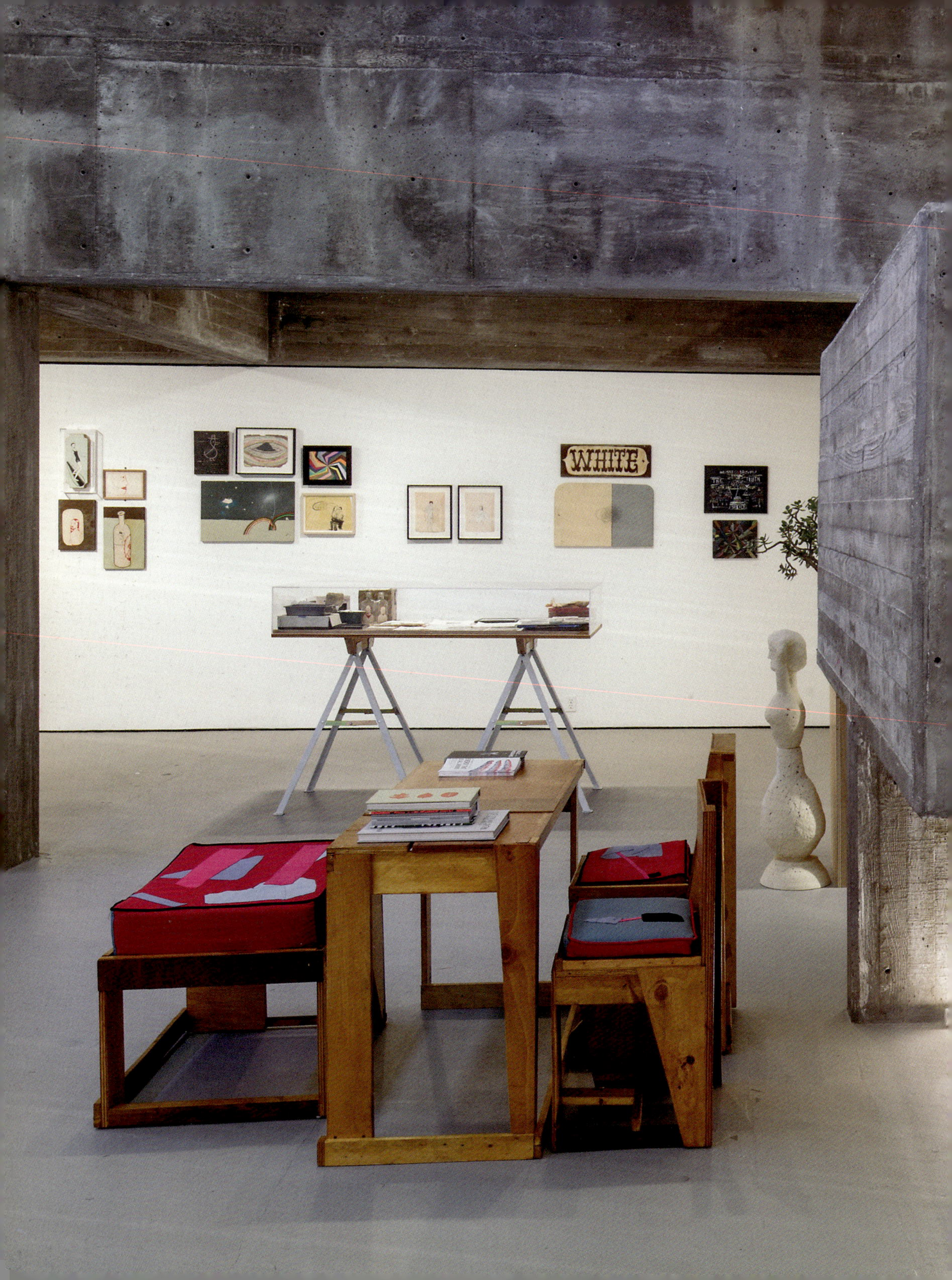
WHITE

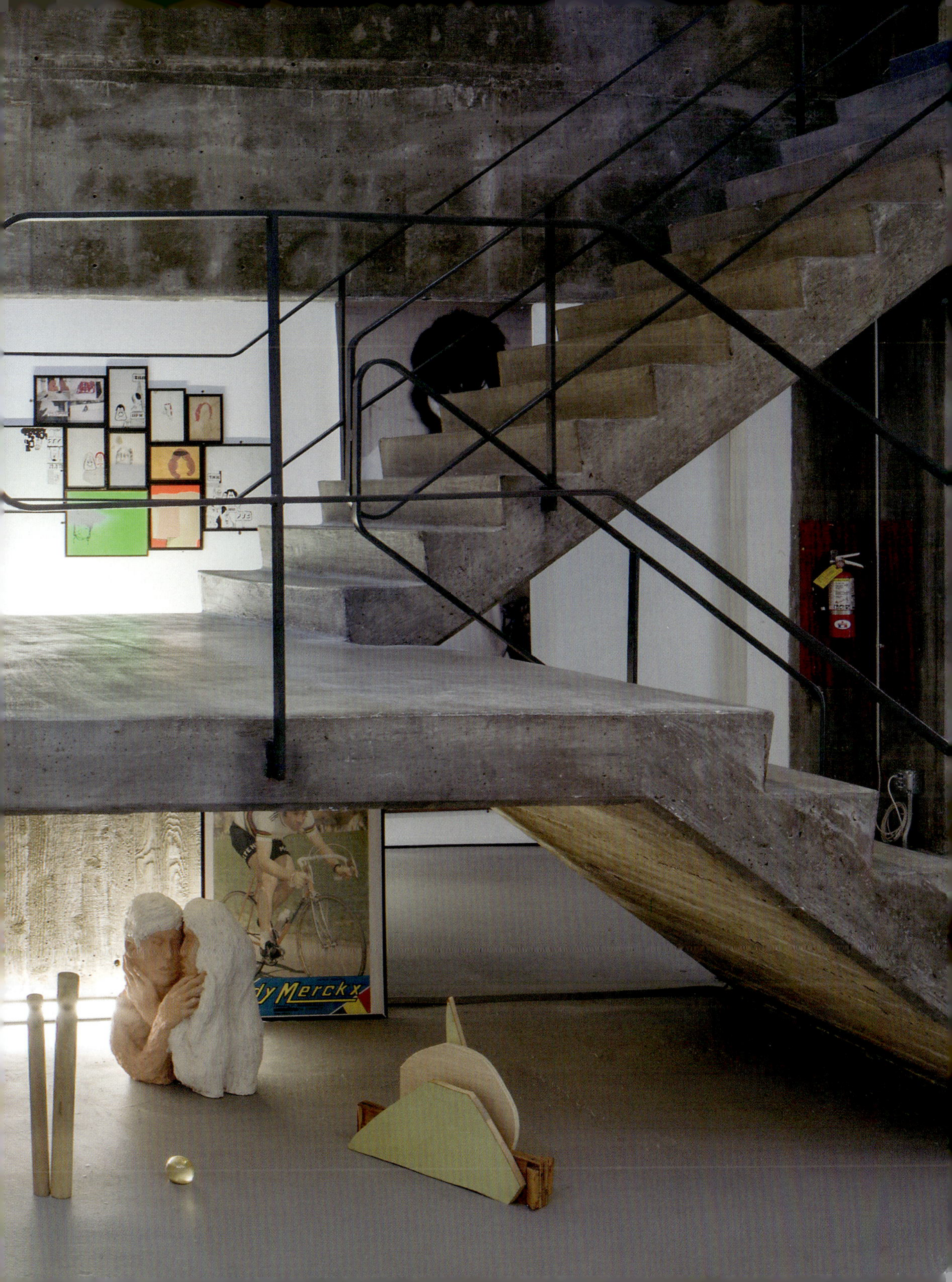
dy Merckx

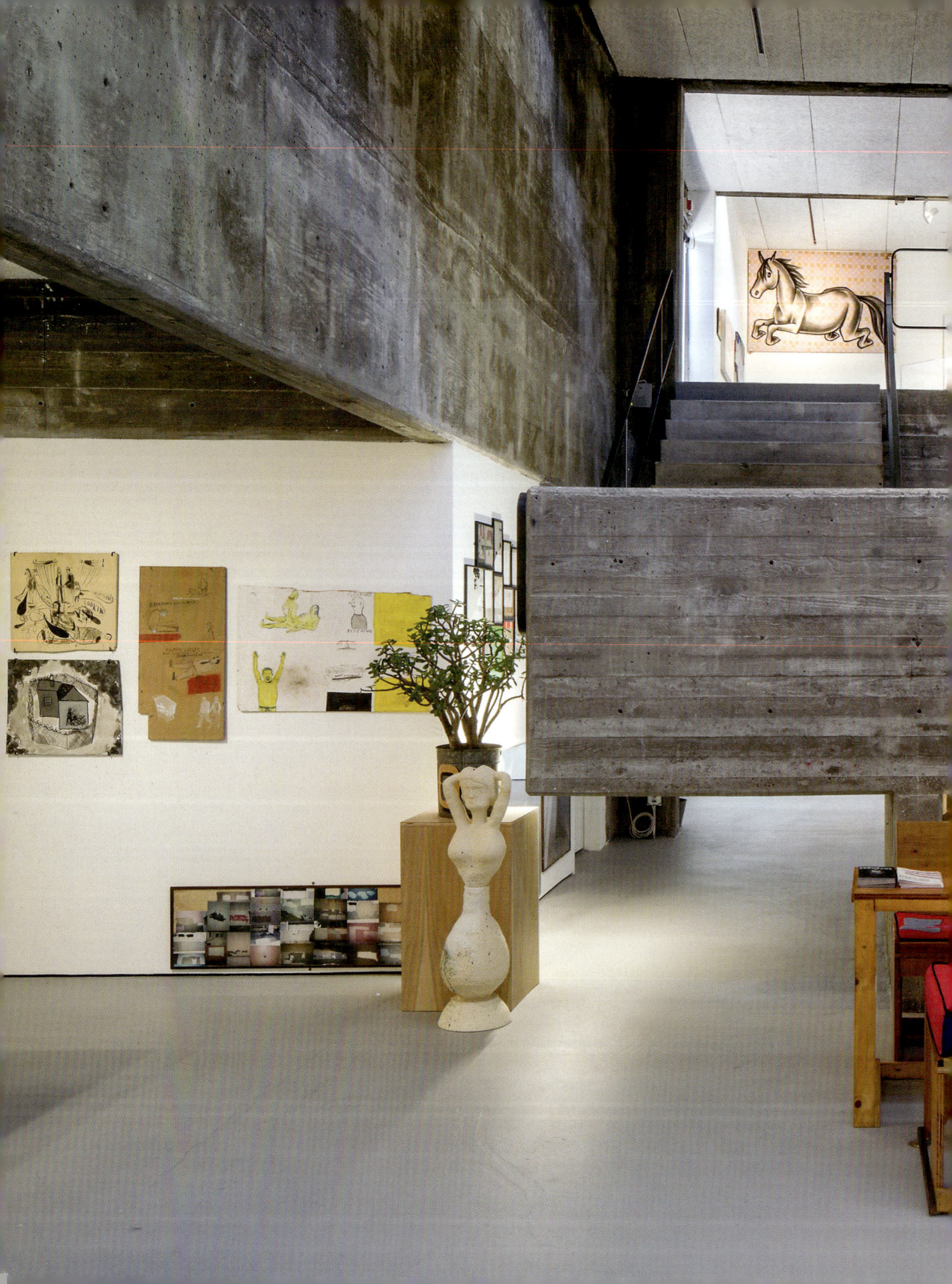

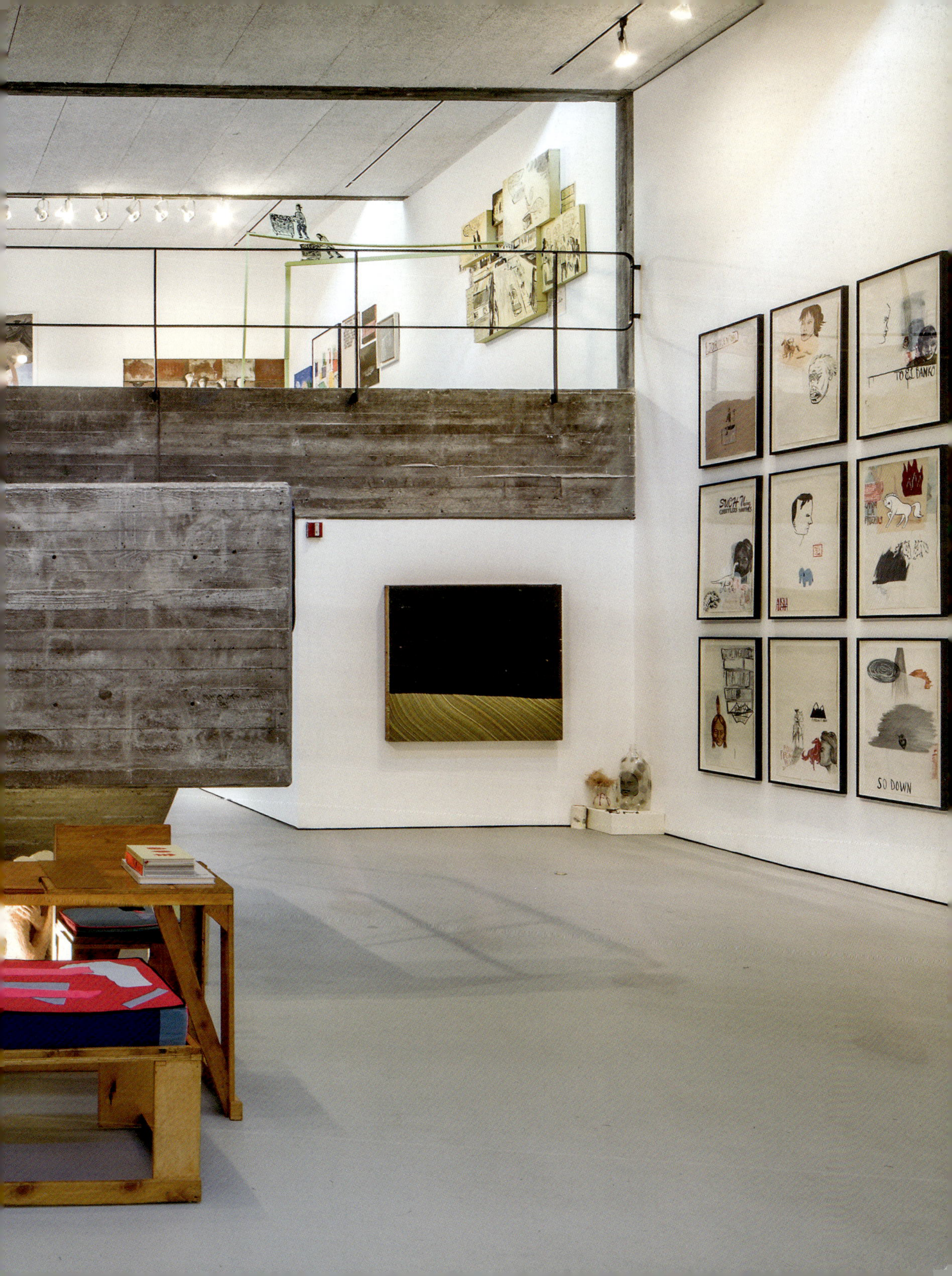
TO EL DANKO
SO DOWN

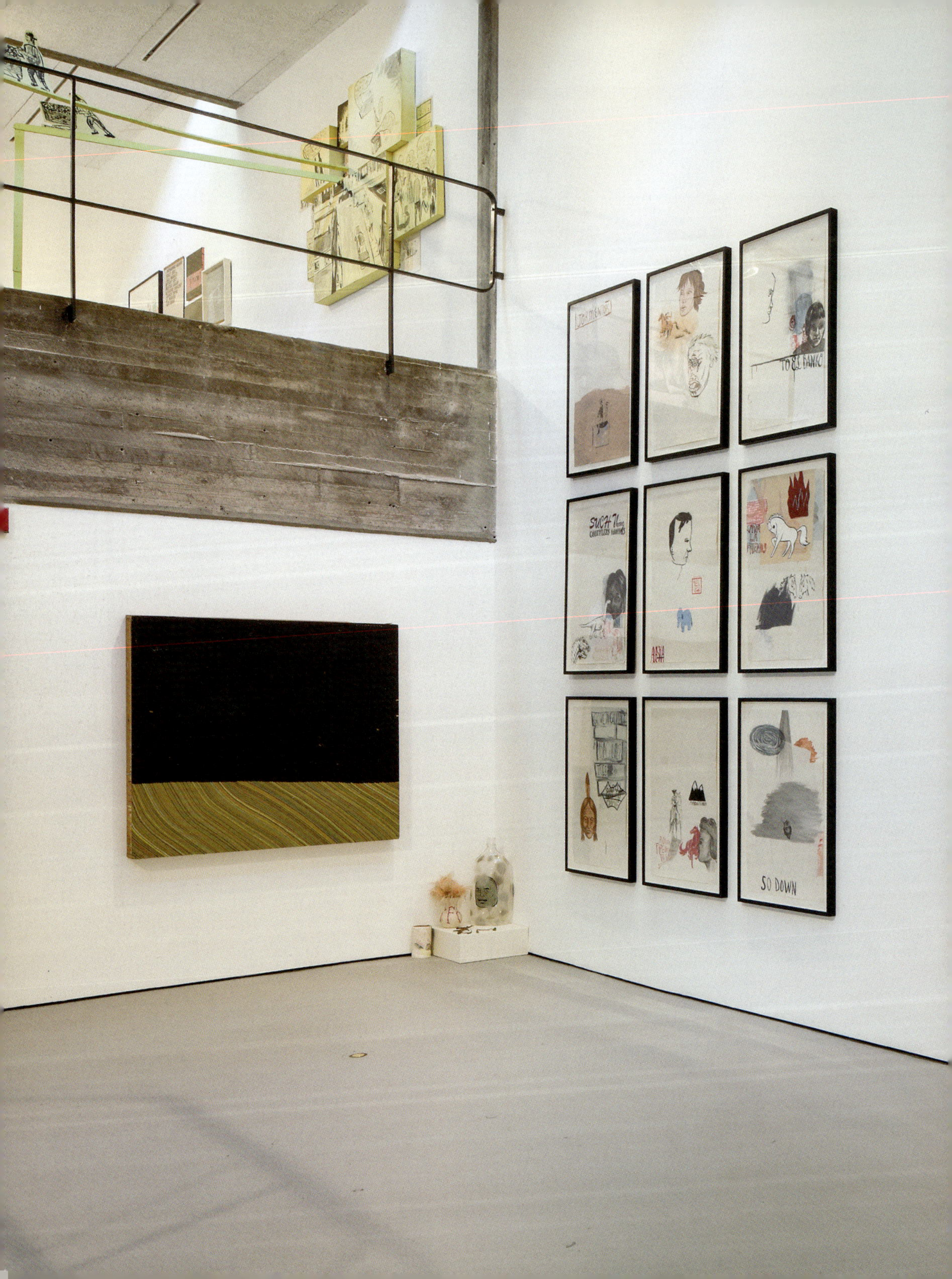
SO DOWN

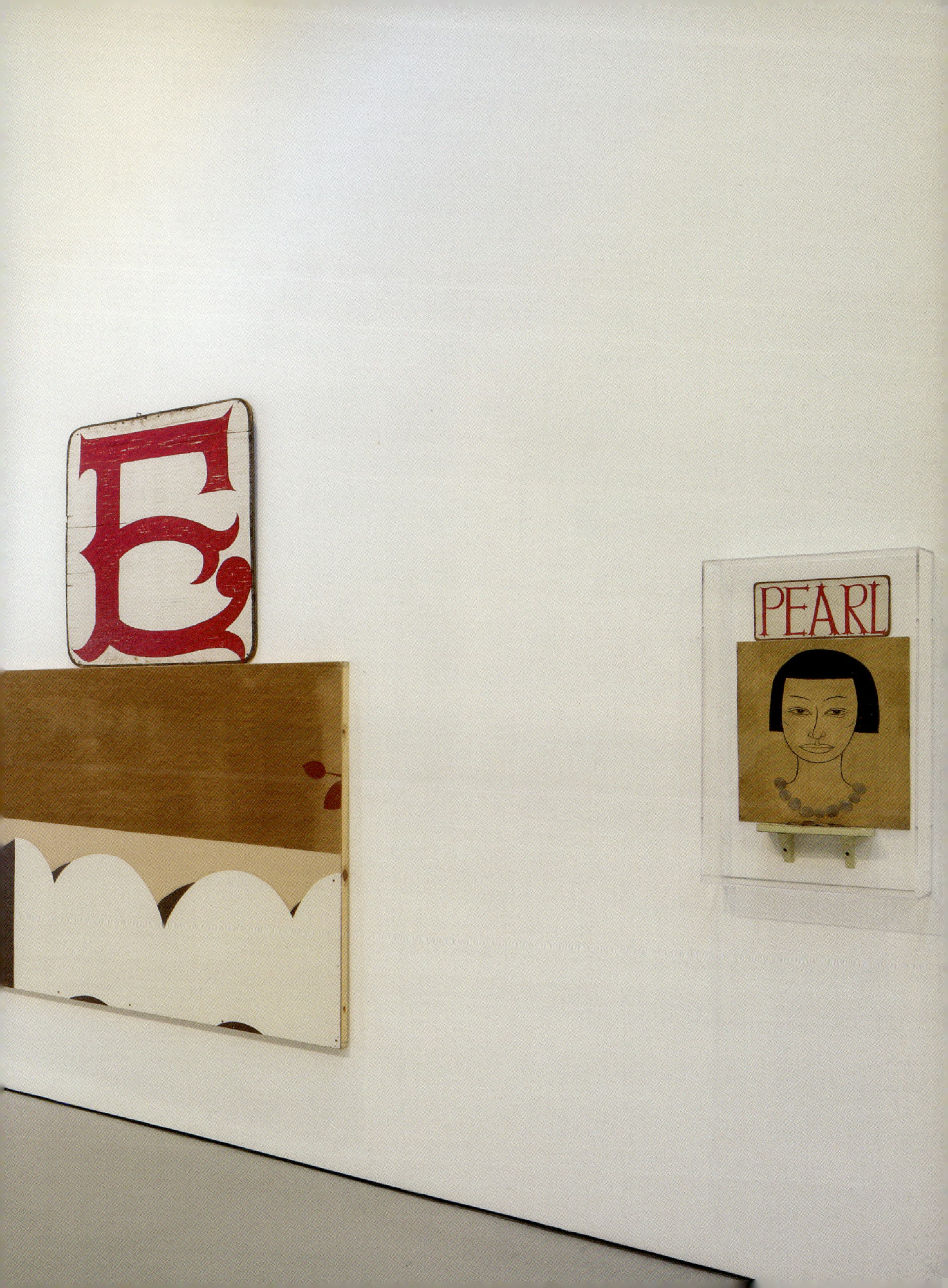
E
PEARL

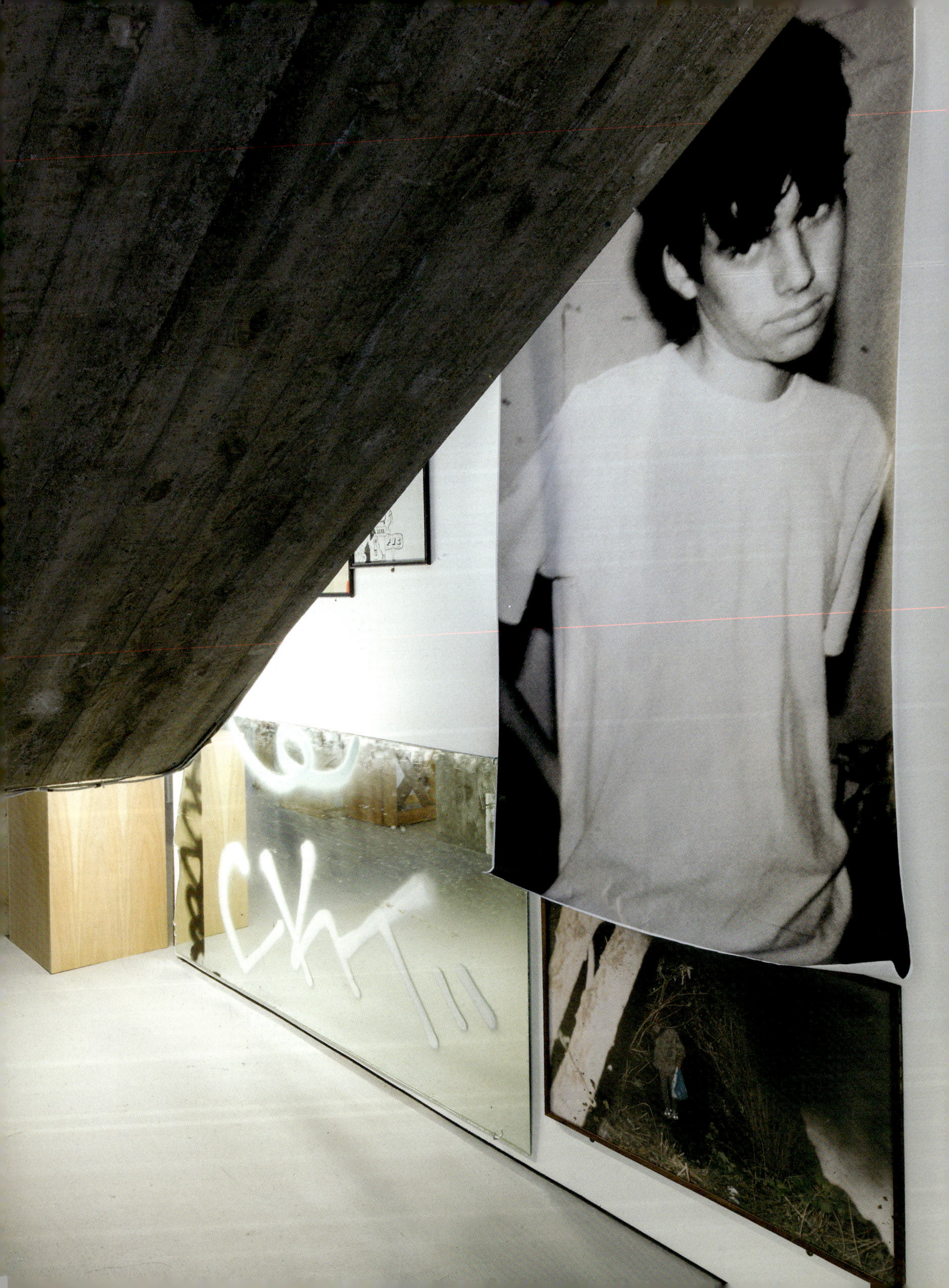

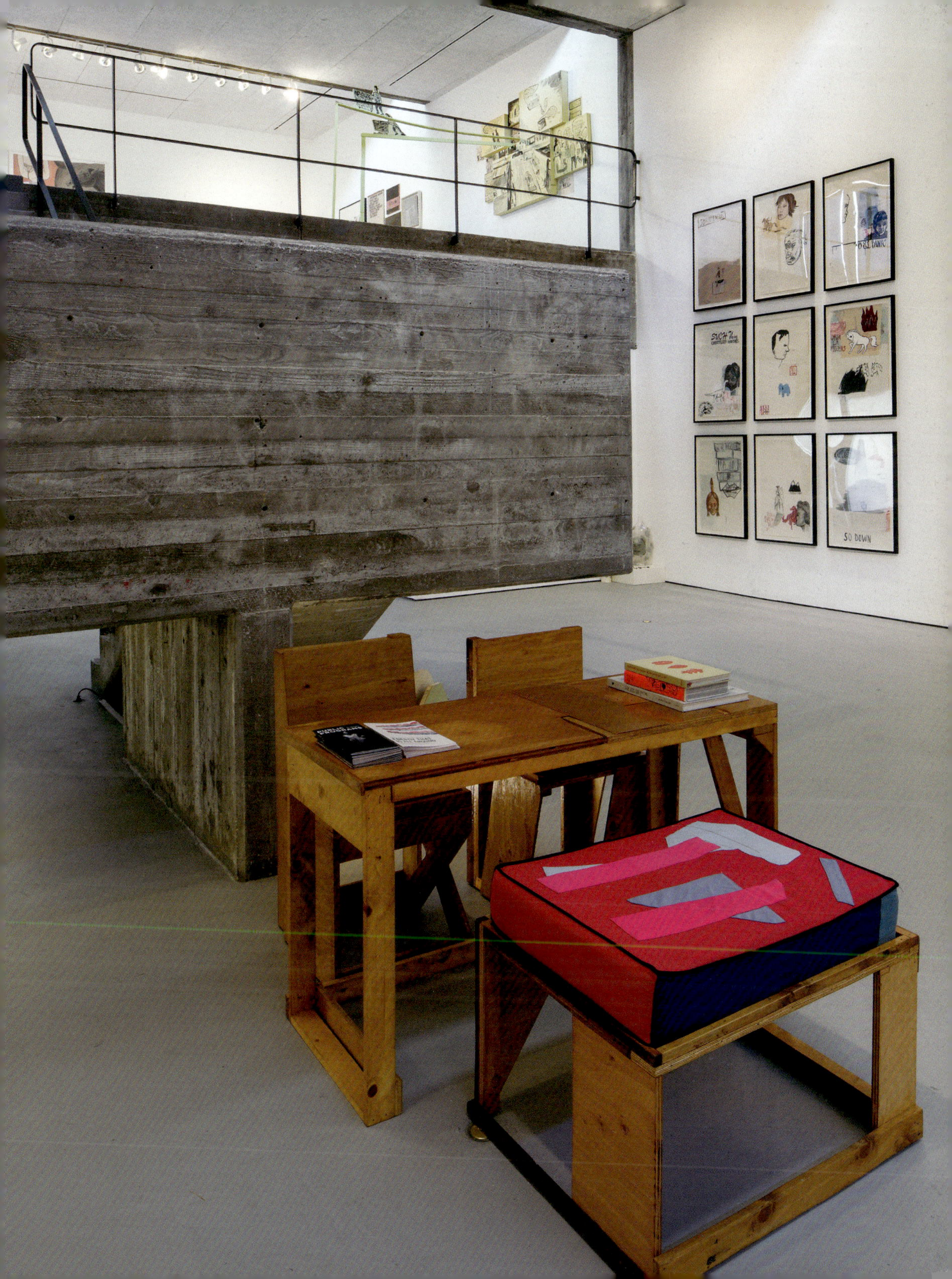
SO DOWN

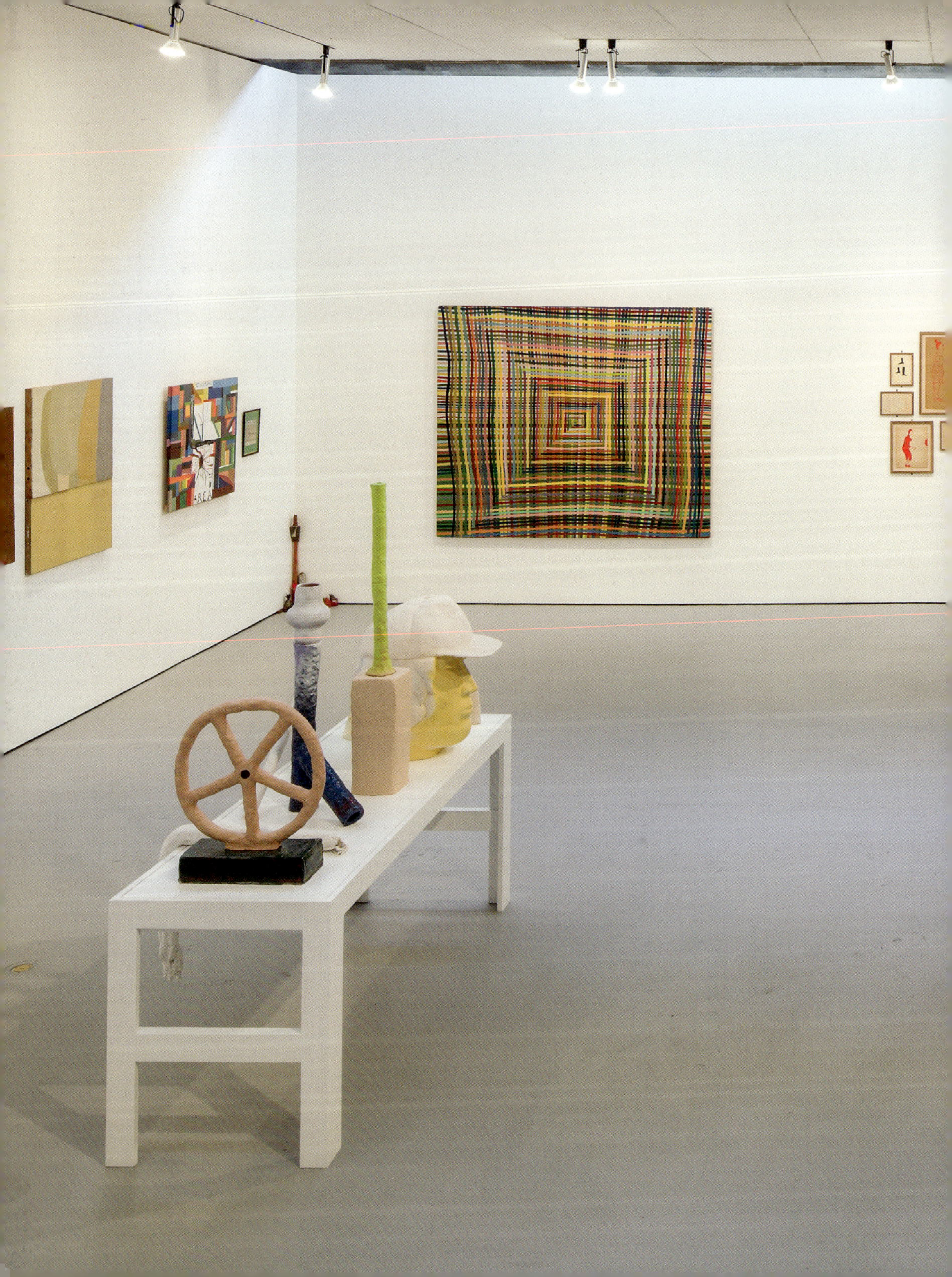

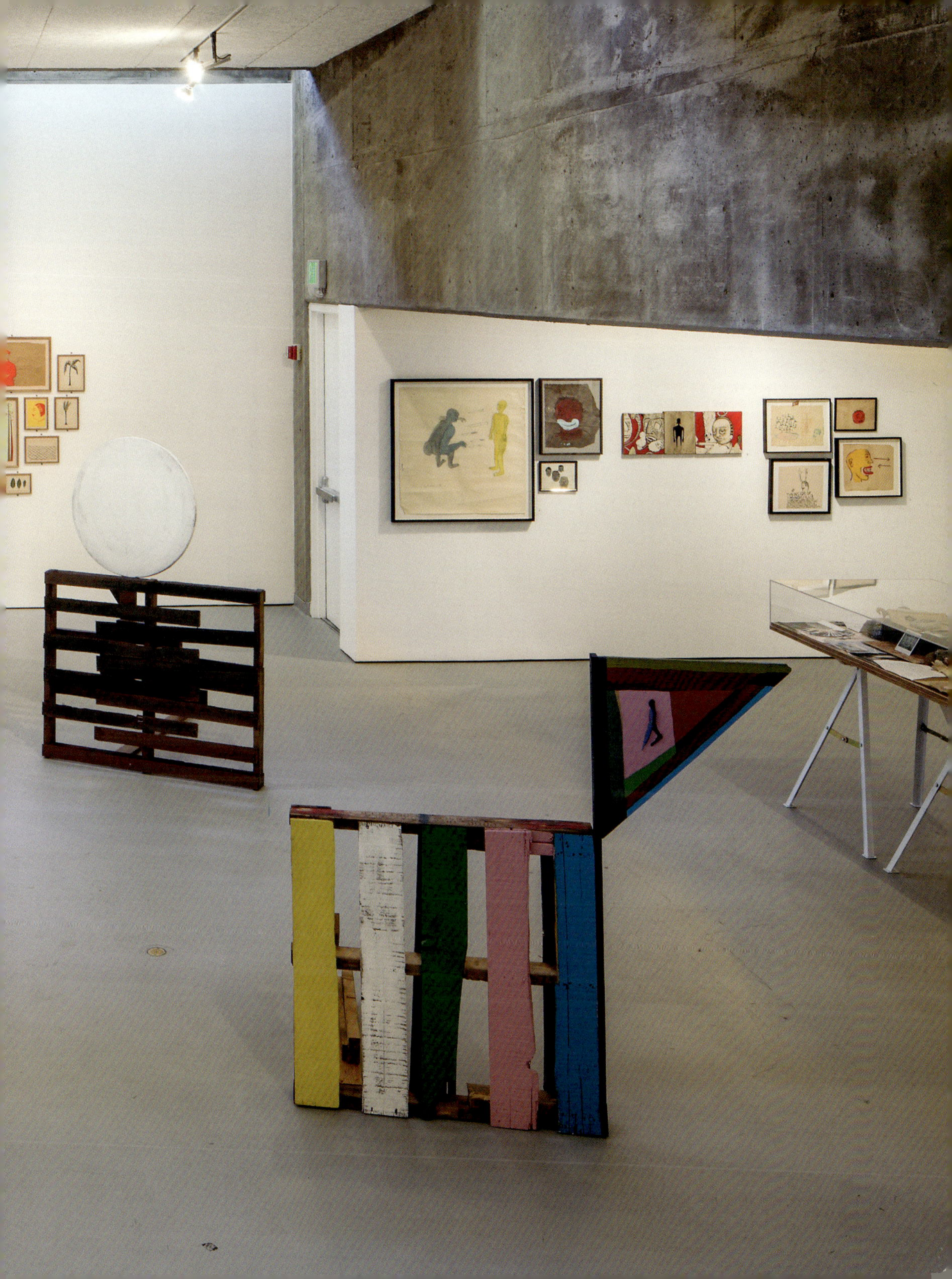

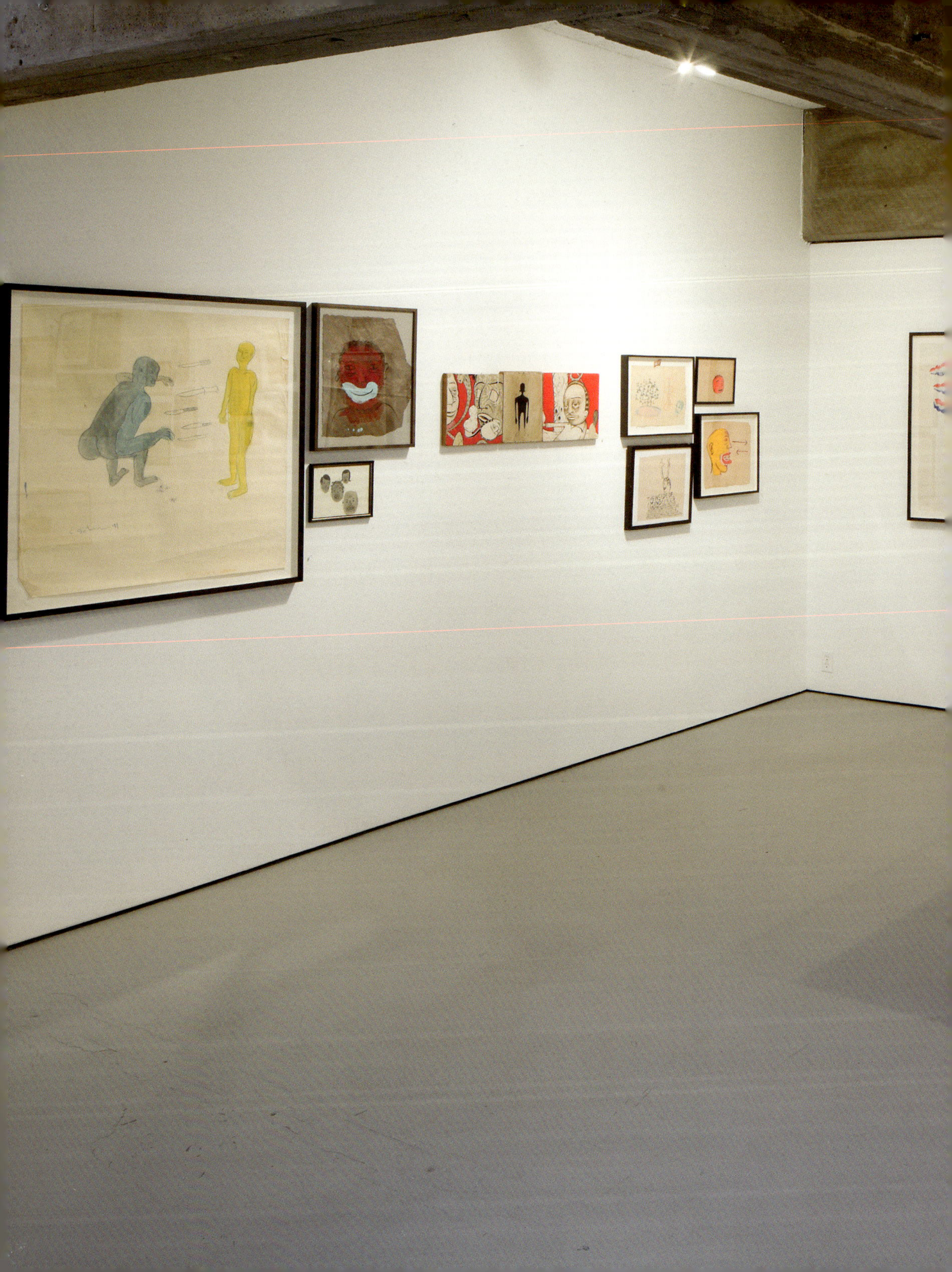

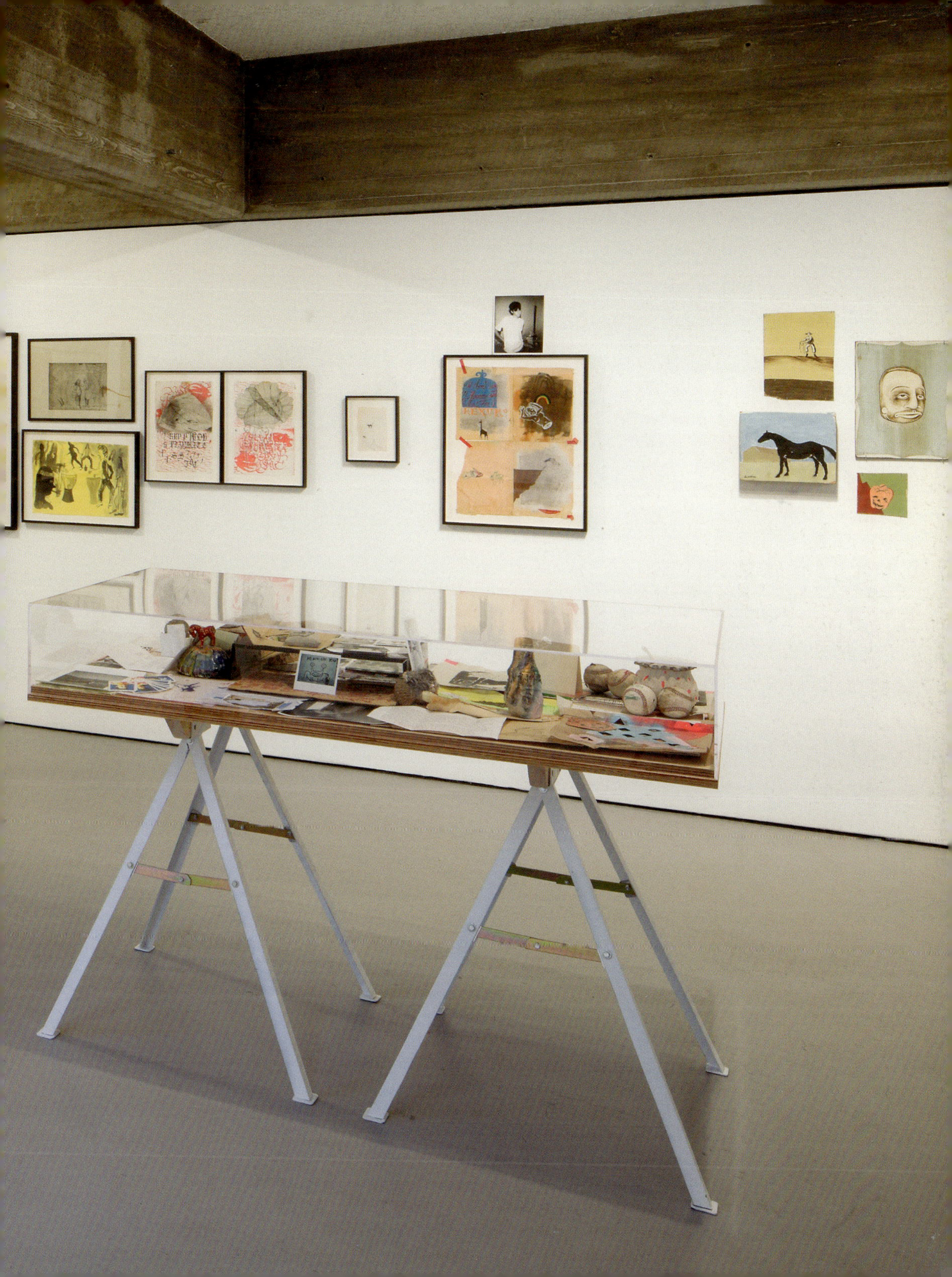

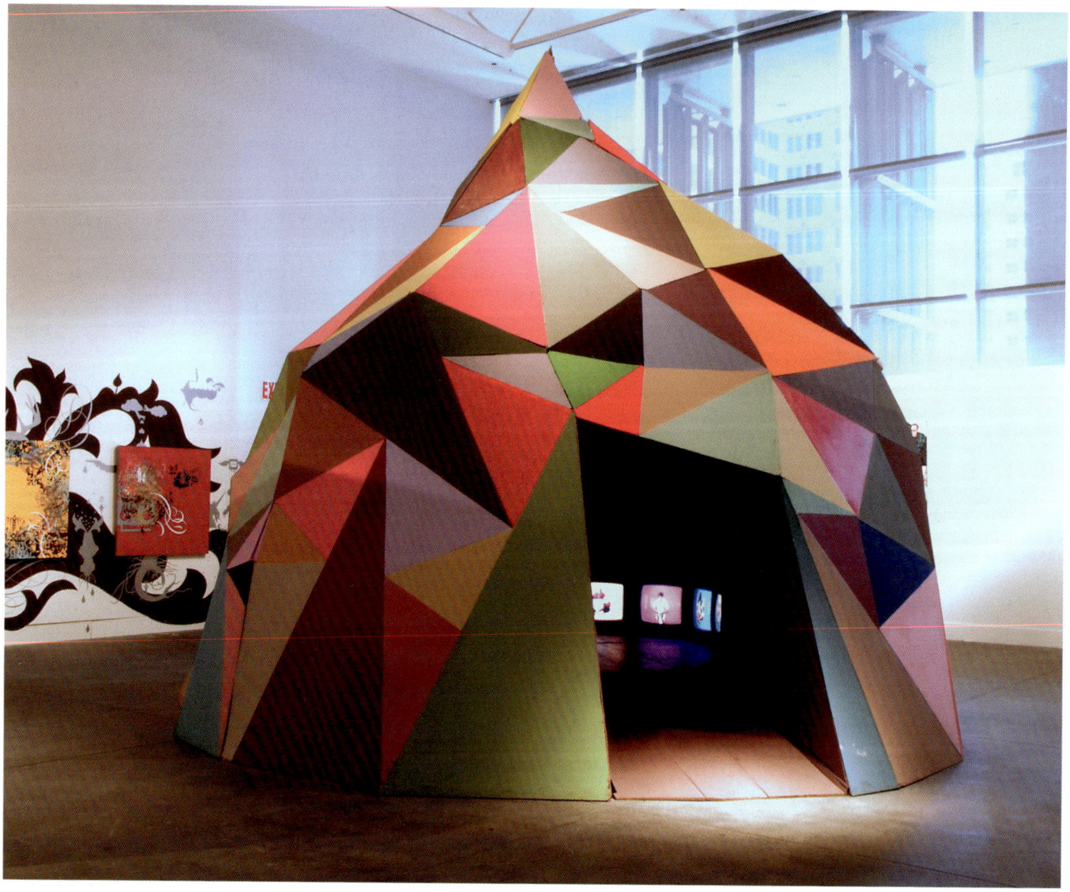

OFF THE TRACKS

Ethics and Aesthetics of Recent San Francisco Art

BY DINA PUGH

AS A YOUNG CURATOR in San Francisco in the early 2000s, I worked with and admired a handful of artists that people sometimes collectively referred to as the Mission School. Juxtaposed against the dot-com boom culture, these artists represented the moral and political voice of our cultural community—a community that was being threatened by gentrification. These artists became well known beyond San Francisco more for their popular "outsider" or "street" appeal, but for me they were political.

I began questioning the term *Mission School* around 2006 when people started using the term freely and often carelessly. I was co-running my own Mission gallery, Triple Base, and directing Jack Hanley's gallery at the time, and we worked heavily with artists who bore that label including Chris Johanson, Jo Jackson, Alicia McCarthy, Keegan McHargue, and Tauba Auerbach.[1] The term was helpful in "marketing" these artists in that it was shorthand to collectors for artists with similar aesthetics, working in a particular place and time. The problem was that this broad label glossed over significant artistic differences while netting in other artists who were tangential to the core ethos of the original group.

CHRIS JOHANSON
UNTITLED *(installation view)*, 2004
Yerba Buena Center for the Arts, San Francisco

Now, seven years later, as I consider the *ENERGY THAT IS ALL AROUND* exhibition of key Mission School artists, I am no longer concerned with the theoretical or academic "usefulness" of labeling a group of artists. I am more curious about how people viewing their work retrospectively conceive of these artists now that their aesthetic has become emulated by so many younger artists, and removed from its early social or political context. I hope that by considering each Mission School artist in the context of the sociopolitical landscape that sparked their work, the nuances of the Mission School appear more diverse than a single label implies.

THE BOOM

In the late 1990s, the dot-com boom brought to San Francisco's Mission District an influx of young professionals, upscale shops and restaurants, threats of eviction, inflated rents, and an oversaturation of billboard advertisements. Previously, the Mission was a primarily working-class, Latino neighborhood with a small population of struggling artists who found the area affordable and inspirational because of its diversity. Between 1990 and 1998, twenty-nine businesses on Valencia between Sixteenth and Eighteenth Streets turned over (more than half of the stores on those blocks). Among the stores that left were a furniture store, a Laundromat, a Salvadoran bakery, and a corner market. Those that moved in included upscale restaurants, a vintage clothing store, and trendy housewares and gift stores.[2] Throughout the city, long-term residents, community-serving local businesses, arts and cultural organizations, and even charter schools were displaced by skyrocketing rents supported by dot-coms with inflated budgets.[3]

The visual transformation of the city was a major source of discontent for artists living in the area.[4] In a PBS documentary, Margaret Kilgallen called billboards "mind garbage," and Barry McGee said that commercial jingles are far more damaging than graffiti, which can easily be painted over.[5] Many other like-minded artists working in the Mission at the same time resisted the influence of new money coming into their neighborhood by privileging the outcast, discarded, and forgotten elements of their urban surroundings and using craft as a protest of digital advancement. The social tension inherent in this gentrification spurred artwork that shared a distinctive urban and cartoonlike style involving found objects, scrap wood, or flat house paint—literally repurposing the discarded markers of development. Beyond this common aesthetic, key to the artists' practice and evident in the choice of materials, was a striving to retain personal integrity and hold close to personal relationships while resisting what the artists perceived to be an increasingly alienating and commercialized world.

"THE MISSION SCHOOL"

Chris Johanson, Margaret Kilgallen, Barry McGee, and Alicia McCarthy are often referred to in the same breath and are understood to be key artists of the Mission School. Since then they have been linked to one another, implying (somewhat inaccurately) that they worked together as a communal group. As small as it is—only twenty blocks long—the Mission contains varied artist subcommunities. Chris Johanson told me that he hadn't even met Barry or Margaret until years after living in the same small neighborhood.[6] Barry McGee and Margaret Kilgallen came from art school backgrounds, and Barry often talks about his connection to the graffiti scene and how integral it is to his art practice. Chris Johanson identifies his "school" as a multidisciplinary group of artists who hung out at Adobe Books and the grassroots galleries ESP, Scene/Escena, and Four Walls, all located near the intersection of Sixteenth Street and Valencia (all now have since closed or been displaced). While Alicia McCarthy knew Barry and Margaret from art school and the graffiti scene, she had closer ties with the queer and punk subculture that held its unofficial headquarters at the Epicenter Zone where Alicia

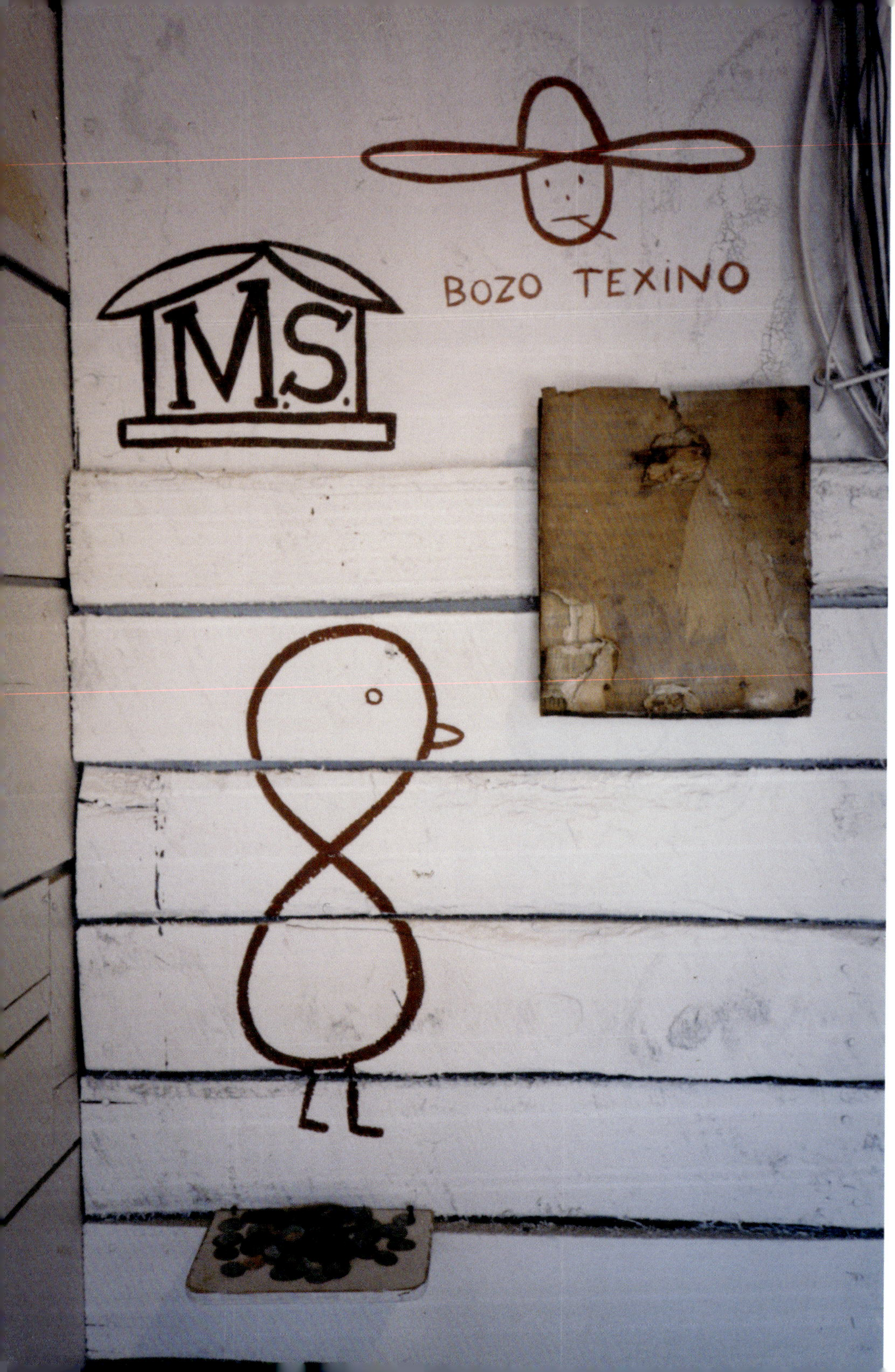
BOZO TEXINO
M.S.

had her studio. Also near the bustling intersection where Chris Johanson most often found himself, Epicenter was a volunteer-operated record, zine, and bookstore, a place for film screenings and art shows, and a meeting point for political activist groups.

While these artists may not have been working side by side, their somewhat overlapping subcultures were bound together by a shared antiestablishment ethos—a politics of resistance that was especially heightened with the threatened collapse of their respective communities. By 2000, the Epicenter Zone had closed for financial reasons, and the gallery directors of ESP, Scene/Escena, and Four Walls all moved to Los Angeles, due to increased rents and their shared perception that San Francisco was turning "unfriendly towards artists."[7]

CHRIS JOHANSON

In a wonderfully animated email exchange, Chris Johanson described to me "his Mission School" as a constellation of people working in varied disciplines such as music, poetry, and documentary film. His closest group of friends was Andrew McKinley, photographer and owner of artist hub Abode Books; Cliff Hengst and Scott Hewicker, both painters and members of the band Troll; painter and video artist Jo Jackson (now Johanson's wife); assemblage artist and DJ Chris Corales; and Amy Franceschini, a media-based visual artist. This convergence of various disciplines is a crucial aspect of Chris's practice that he refers to as "documentary painting."[8] He is perhaps best known for his cityscapes filled with everyman stick figures speaking universal truths from cartoon bubbles, and his work is a celebration of multiplicity that earnestly comments on existential issues of human identity compromised by consumer culture.

A seminal piece that Chris and his crew of friends created while I was working at Yerba Buena Center for the Arts in 2004 was his *Untitled* wooden hut/video installation in the exhibition *Beautiful Losers: Contemporary Art and*

MARGARET KILGALLEN
Installation view, 1997–98
Soap Factory, Minneapolis

Street Culture. In the piece, Chris brings together varied individuals from his community into a video drum circle. Monitors form a semicircle, each portraying a bare-chested or primitively clothed drummer beating a hand drum at two-minute intervals. The drummers seem cynical, jaded by the adverse changes that the world has undergone since a previous generation fought for an end to war and for environmental causes in the 1960s.

In Chris's own words: "The drum circle piece is about dealing with all this capitalist modern death negative energy that is coming down on us. We need to coexist. So it is a modern death geodesic dome. All the colors are of the consumer choices that bombard us as well as signifying the magic of life and possibilities. The people are all separate but together beating to there [*sic*] own beat but also together with the human race beat."[9]

The virtual drum circle is housed within a multicolored dome that recalls Buckminster Fuller's geodesic dome, a utopian invention that once promised sustainable living and thereby an end to poverty and future environmental crises.[10] First built by Chris and friends in Cincinnati's Contemporary Arts Center's new gallery space, the dome is fabricated with plywood, two-by-fours, and flat paint salvaged from their previous venue. Chris describes Dumpster-diving for raw materials as a daily routine and even an "obsession."[11] Employing the detritus of architectural structures, he spins Fuller's theory into a comment on the superfluous waste that humans leave behind while optimistically showing that items perceived as refuse can be refashioned into useful structures or even high art. Like the video installation within, Johanson's dome summons utopian ideals of sustainability that are undervalued by mainstream culture in favor of shortsighted capitalist advancement.

With scrappy resourcefulness, Chris Johanson creates his own safe haven for creative production. While his drummers convey the somewhat apathetic attitude held by many of their generation, Chris's work proposes a mini-utopia, one literally constructed with the recycled scraps of consumer culture and built on the connectivity between people of different creative backgrounds.

BARRY McGEE

Barry McGee—aka "Twist," his graffiti pseudonym—references past political movements in his work and is more antagonistic in his approach than Chris Johanson. In a 2004 interview McGee recalled,

> I remember that growing up I used to see a group of activists, The Revolutionary Communist Party (RCP), who would spray-paint aggressive statements on Bank of America, government buildings, and freeway underpasses. They shed light on atrocities being committed by the Reagan administration's policies in El Salvador, Nicaragua, Cuba and so on. I like that—the rawness of it. The stuff that people do now doesn't antagonize anyone at all. It has become like mural art, which is fine in its own right but doesn't anger people when they see it."[12]

To Barry, graffiti is a political act of free expression that asserts the individual's right to communicate within public space—a challenge to sanctioned billboards and advertisements that he says "are sickening to me. I'm disgusted by the culture of desire and consumption, having to have this object, or this product, to better yourself."[13]

In Barry McGee's *One More Thing* installation at Deitch Projects, shockingly bright signs, a pileup of trashed cars, and a near-deafening video and sound installation created a sense of disruption on par with the intensity of the RCP activists. While Barry distances himself from activism by taking up art as his means of expression, the installation stands as a protest, an imagining of a reclaimed visual environment. The documentary photography of fellow taggers and delicately hand-drawn faces of hobos create tiny vibrant communities within his clustered frame installations and on the pages of his zines. Barry's vision embraces the outcasts of society, including his graffiti friends, drunkards, and nomads. He creates a raucous environment that communicates his struggle to retain personal interconnectedness under financially and philosophically threatening conditions. Informing all of Barry McGee's methods of art making is a privileging of human relationships and self-made culture.

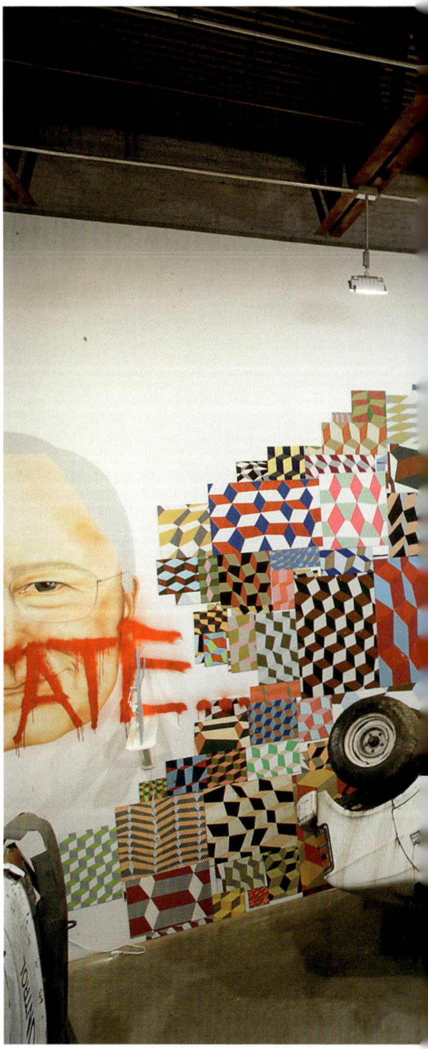

Craig Garrett defined the "professional naïve" as "someone who can channel the visionary transcendence of the social outcast while remaining integrated in the art community and, to a lesser extent, society at large."[14] You can see how Barry channels the outcast in his installation *One More Thing*, where mechanical robots mimic the act of tagging within the gallery. A motorized wax reproduction of Barry's frequent collaborator Josh Lazcano holds a spray can that swings back and forth in repetitive motion suggesting the marking of "Amaze" (Josh's graffiti alias) onto a presprayed wall. Barry does not bring graffiti into the gallery. Rather he points to the almost laughable attempt to re-create the conditions of the street within private space—a contradiction that he felt was unresolved in the graffiti-inspired art of the '80s.[15] When working in a gallery setting, Barry McGee doesn't use his street name "Twist," but his alter ego "Ray Fong," a stereotypical Asian-American cartoon-like figure pointing to the artist's cultural identity. This identity switch suggests that Barry works in two different modes: one when he is tagging "throw-ups" on the street and another when he is considering full installations in the gallery space. He is aware of the different interpretations that his work takes on within an art context, and this sophistication is what differentiates Barry from so many other graffiti artists or muralists who merely re-create their work from the street inside the gallery.

In the same Deitch Projects show, Barry stacked the life-size wax figurines of his friends tagging a wall alongside

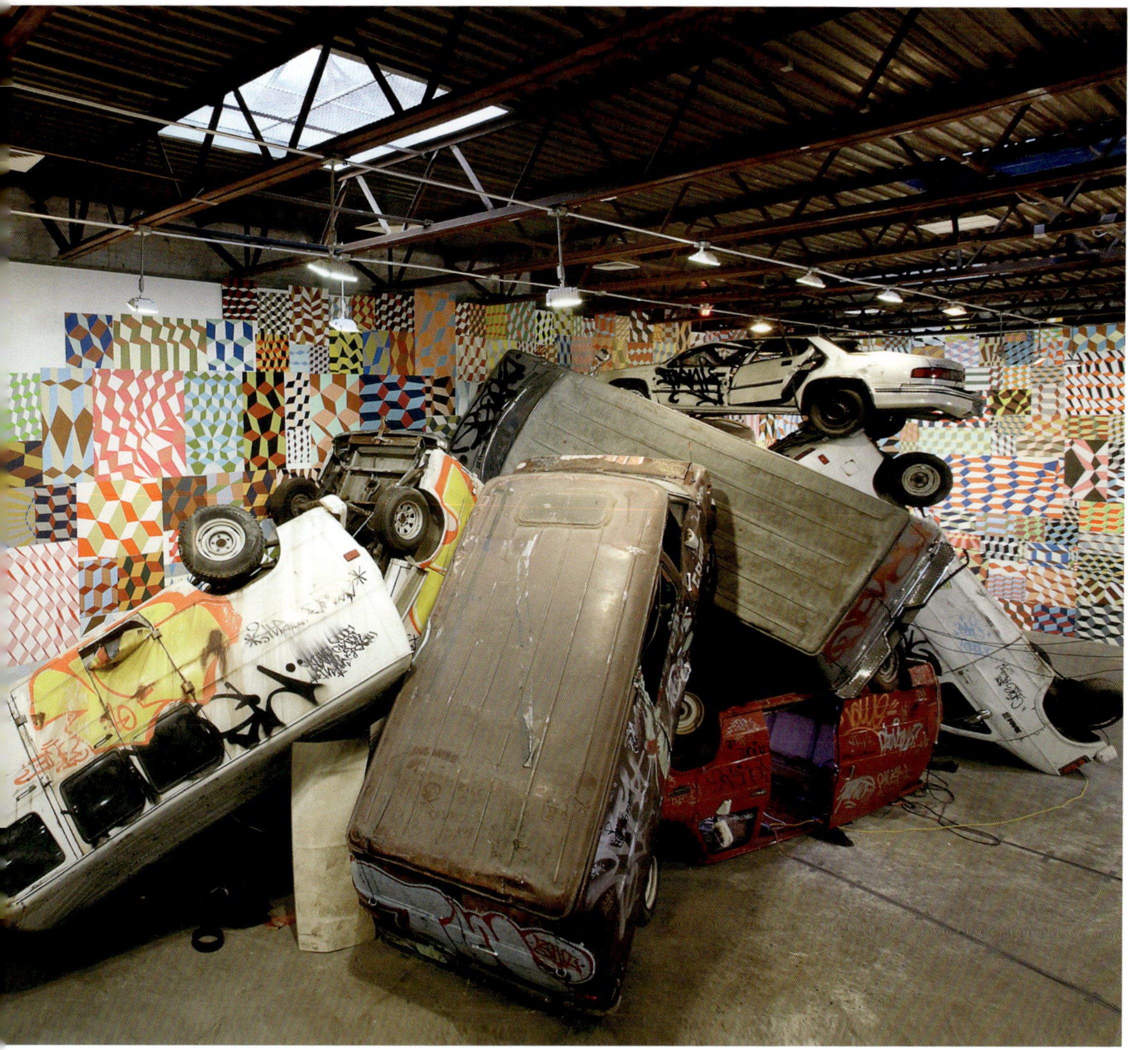

BARRY McGEE
ONE MORE THING
(installation view), 2005
Deitch Projects, New York

a carved wooden totem pole also spray-painting a black cloud onto the opposite wall. He connects graffiti to a long lineage of cultural production, as a primitive act of mark making that stems from the earliest cave drawings. Thrift store picture frames, found bottles, old TV sets, and VCRs provide the canvases for Barry's imagery and summon a more recent legacy of artists—from the surrealists to the '50s' and '60s' assemblage artists—who similarly recycled detritus and challenged moral and aesthetic hierarchies. For the show, Barry McGee and his circle of friends also produced a zine called *Larceny*—a cheaply produced staple-bound collection of Xeroxed photographs documenting their street tags and police citations that also has precedents in previous underground movements from dadaism to punk.

An inherent conflict for a "professional naïve" such as Barry is that while the artwork is imbedded in an anti-institutional or anticapitalist philosophy, it's nearly impossible to have a career as a working artist while remaining outside of an art institution or the art market. In fact, cultural institutions and galleries have a vested interest in occasionally shining attention on artists such as Barry and his peers to reaffirm their own antiestablishment currency. Barry has expressed his discomfort with altering his work so that it may be preserved to enter museum or personal collections. However, for the most part, he has conceded and works frequently on large wooden panels rather than directly onto the wall so that his pieces can be preserved, stored, and reinstalled. He admitted early in his career in 2001: "What I do is definitely tainted. It's a contradiction."[16] Since then he has gone on to appear in major museums and art fairs internationally and become the art market's most popular artist of his generation from the region.

Around 2005, Barry McGee began changing up his largely figurative signature style, as seen in the juxtaposition of two similar cluster installations made in 2000 and 2005. Both were installed in the same corner at Deitch Projects gallery in New York, one for an early show, *Street Market* (2000), and the other, five years later, for *One More Thing* (2005). The *Street Market* installation consisted primarily of photographs, figurative drawings, and pieces of larger murals depicting the droopy-eyed, downtrodden hobos who make up Barry's cityscape. His signature faces are scarcely found in the *One More Thing* installation. Rather, Barry introduces a plethora of geometrical neon panels made in mass quantities by a crew of gallery interns. These forms create a psychedelic optical illusion—the visual equivalent of the chaotic sound installation—that dominates most of the walls of the first tier of the gallery and creeps into the cluster work on the second level. Barry speaks to his shift away from the figurative:

> [There] was a time in graffiti when it was fun to do images. In hindsight, it opened the floodgates to tons of terrible art school graffiti and non-abrasive images. I have come full circle and now condemn images and praise the fundamental graffiti acts of tags and throw-ups on everything . . . but I'm getting tired of iconography now and am fighting to get rid of it. I came close in Cincinnati. There was only one painting that included figures, and it got stolen, so the show went back to containing no imagery at all.[17]

Barry McGee has asserted a new direction in his work, one that downplays the individual figure. Recalling the colors and geometric patterns of Chris Johanson's geodesic dome structure, Barry also references the increasing saturation of visually seductive, yet manipulative, imagery in contemporary urban life.

ALICIA McCARTHY

Like her contemporaries, Alicia McCarthy works mostly with recycled materials, Dumpster-diving for supplies in impoverished areas like San Francisco's Hunters Point (once used as a navy shipyard and now home to hundreds of artists' studios and low-income families). In Alicia's

The Forgoton Works, which was part of her untitled 2003 exhibition at the Jack Hanley Gallery, the corner piece is constructed of resurrected scrap wood covered in matte house paint, also Chris Johanson's materials of choice. Her color selections—muted greens, oranges, grays, and blues—evoke the recent military presence in the disused shipyard. The ambiguously shaped plywood pieces stacked against the wall can read as silhouettes of overflowing paint buckets and piles of wood arranged haphazardly as in an artist's studio or a construction site. A triangular wooden platform wedged against the corner serves as a stage for a scattering of constructed and found objects including a cartoonlike hammer lodged into the platform (further implying a scene of manual labor or artistic production), a large rubber band ball, and a pinecone covered in green paint. The pinecone seems out of place, just teetering on the edge of the platform as if it could be knocked off with the slightest touch. Its precariousness implies a subtle connection to the natural environment that is so easily lost in the rush of city living and rapid advancement for which the leftover wood serves as a reminder.

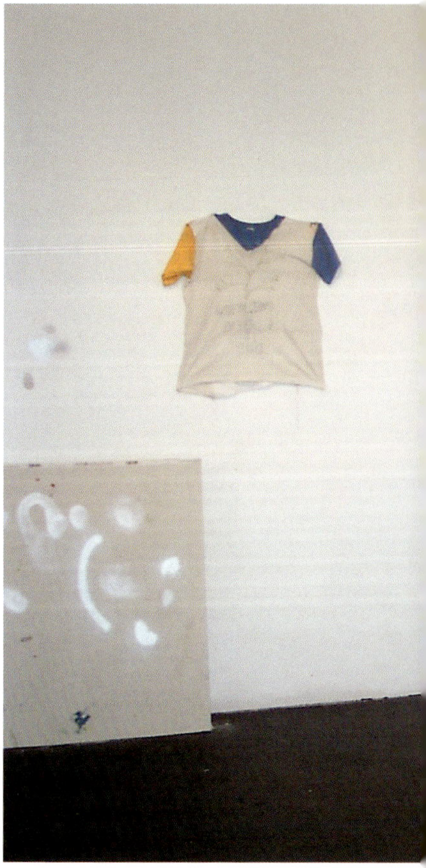

Alicia McCarthy's connection (or disconnection) to the natural environment is equally as present in this corner piece as her relationship to urban culture. The edge of the installation is irreverently spritzed with red spray paint, perhaps an afterthought from the phrase "The Forgoton Works" spray-painted high above the wooden assemblage. Like Barry, Alicia's use of graffiti connects her work within the gallery to her street identity; her monikers are "Fancy" and "Probe."[18] Alicia's art school education and formal acuity are apparent in her skillful use of color and assemblage and then juxtaposed by her messy graffiti sensibility honed through her education on the street. This duality seems to insist on a connection between her outsider (read "forgoton") identity as a queer punk involved in an underground culture and her role as an artist in the public sphere.

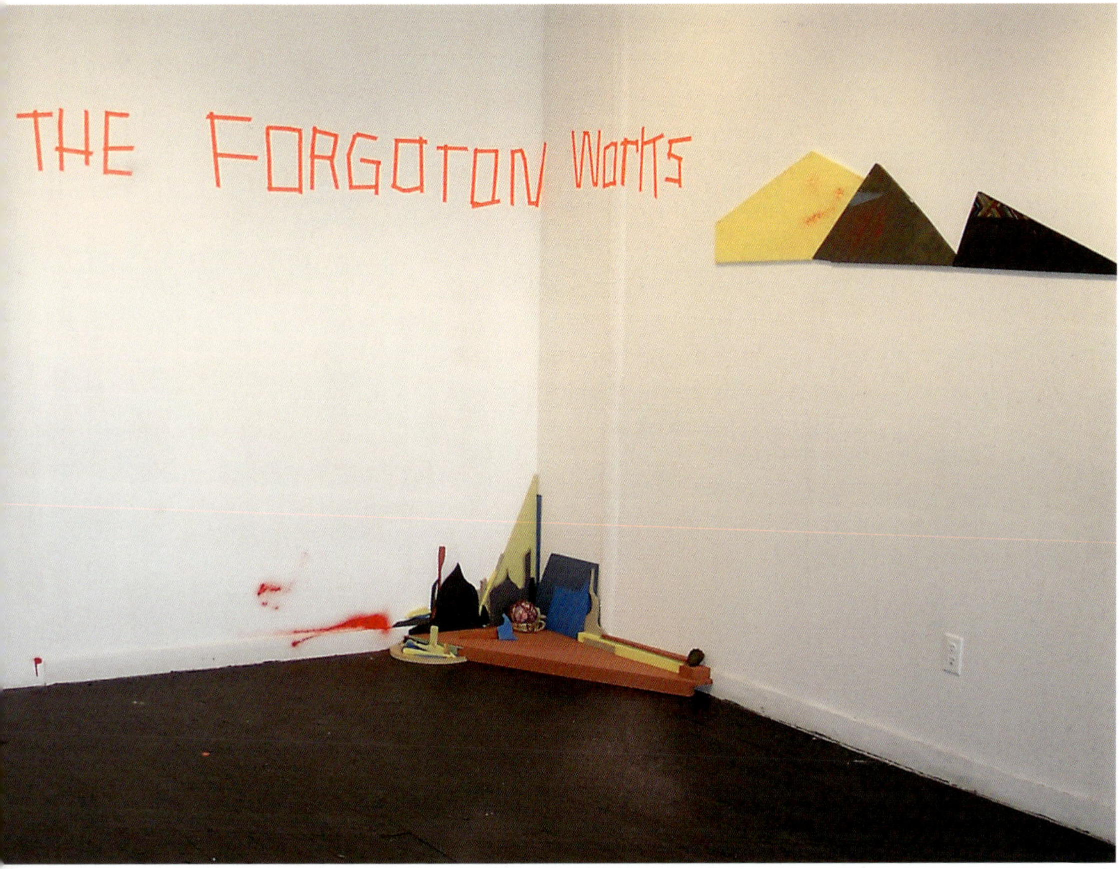

ALICIA McCARTHY
THE FORGOTON WORKS
(installation view), 2003
Jack Hanley Gallery,
San Francisco

Alicia McCarthy's graffiti text "Forgoton" emblazed over the corner piece and her reverence of discarded materials can also be interpreted as an homage to her recently dismantled artist community. This corner piece was sited at the Jack Hanley Gallery, which moved from its downtown location to the Mission District in 2000 right after spaces like the Epicenter Zone punk collective were forced out just down the street. Alicia's exhibition, which also incorporated works by her graffiti artist friends such as Sara Thustra (aka "Heart" or "Z"), attempts to bring back a spirit of collectivity and antiestablishment activity that was fostered in her former studio and home base.

Perhaps in an attempt to exist outside of the capitalist system, Alicia spent three years (on and off) living and working in the small Northern California town of Willits, trading her manual labor for a cabin with no electricity or phone access. Alicia is more concerned with living consistently with her political views and leaving as much time as possible for exploring her art practice than promoting her work publicly, which may partially explain why she has not become as well known as the other artists who were likewise placed under the umbrella of Mission School. She has rarely shown in commercial galleries[19] and thus has retained her outsider status and remained consistent with the subversive ethos embedded in the artwork.

While Barry McGee and Chris Johanson have paved the way for future artists from the region to show in large institutional or commercial gallery settings outside the Bay Area, Alicia McCarthy is equally as influential to emerging artists who look to her as a model for remaining on the fringes of the institutional and commercial sectors of the art world. Younger artists often cite her work, primarily pattern-based and abstract since her departure from figuration in art school, as an inspiration, and visual similarities can be seen in much of the work coming out of the area today.

POST-BOOM SHIFTS

Jo Jackson, an artist who worked in the Mission District from the mid '90s until she moved in 2004, explained to me: "There was a time when I felt very, very connected to a lot of artists in SF. So much that I really felt like we were practically scientists working toward something all together."[20] The close working relationships Jo described have since been thrown into disarray after the loss of so many galleries, institutions, and artists to more affordable cities. At the same time, these adverse conditions also gave the artists something to push against, a political cause to rally around and subvert in their work.

Looking closely at the work being produced now in the Bay Area, it seems that something has been lost, but equally important, a new perspective has been gained. The anti-institutional sensibility, the privileging of one's community in the closest sense of the word, has been fading away along with the figuration and text that once served as its marker. Emerging artists are also more willing to take their work outside of their local context and even relocate in the face of an ever-growing art market, not to mention the highest rents the Bay Area has ever seen, which has forced artists to work harder at selling their work or to move.

Mission School helps define the spirit of art making and a distinctive style that arose from the Mission District in the mid to late '90s. However, the geographical reference of the term is increasingly problematic, with so many artists today moving from coast to coast and relocating from the Mission to cheaper parts of the Bay Area. The only unarguable definition of *Mission School* is a particular group of artists making work at a certain time and place for similar reasons. More expansively, *Mission School* could be understood not as a "movement" but as a shared ethos, and then it can extend to countless others who are similarly engaged in this art of resistance.

1 Keegan and Tauba were younger than the original Mission School artists, but many people still spoke about them as the "new wave" of Mission School artists, although the artists themselves resisted the label and wanted to be defined individually. I would agree, considering the content and form of the work, that neither really fit in the category. However, Keegan's flat painting, with its cartoonlike aesthetic, has certain parallels with Chris Johanson and Barry McGee, and Tauba does seem to be influenced by Alicia's op-art aesthetic. Tauba's early text-based work, related to her early career as a sign painter, is also reminiscent of Margaret Kilgallen's homages to sign painting.

2 Angela Rowen and Gabriel Roth, "The Mission: Lofts and Lattes," *San Francisco Bay Guardian*, October 7, 1998.

3 One indicator of gentrification in the Mission District is the inordinate share of owner move-in evictions (OMIs). More than 16 percent of the city's OMIs occurred in the 94110 zip code from 1997 to 1999, even though the Mission has only 9 percent of the city's rental units. Forty percent of the OMIs that occurred during the entire decade occurred in 1998 alone.

Another indicator was the increase of average rents in the Mission District compared to the rest of San Francisco from 1997 to 1999. The average rent of a two-bedroom unit in the Mission District rose by 26 percent, while the average rent of a two-bedroom unit in San Francisco rose only 16 percent over the same period. Simon Velasquez Alejandrino, *Gentrification in San Francisco's Mission District: Indicators and Policy Recommendations* (San Francisco: Mission Economic Development Association, Summer 2000).

4 The "17 Reasons" sign stood atop a building at Seventeenth and Mission since 1935 when it originally read "17 Reasons Why," a slogan for Redlick's Furniture Store, which closed in 1975. It was a landmark that symbolized the endurance of the Mission's spirit to withstand the drastic changes that came at the end of the 1990s. In 2002, it was removed and replaced by a Miller Genuine Draft ad, causing uproar in the neighborhood and media attention. Laurel Wellman, "Much Ado about Mission District's 17 Reasons," *San Francisco Chronicle*, June 25, 2002.

5 Margaret Kilgallen and Barry McGee, "Barry McGee and Margaret Kilgallen," *Art21: Art in the Twenty-First Century* (Alexandria, VA: PBS Home Video, 2001).

6 Chris Johanson, interview by Dina Pugh, February 23, 2006.

7 Jesse Hamlin, "Heading Out of Town: Artists leave San Francisco for less expensive digs in New York, Los Angeles and even Wonder Valley," *San Francisco Chronicle*, October 19, 2000.

8 Chris Johanson, "Fame: on the streets with installation artist Chris Johanson," *Spark* (San Francisco: KQED Public Television and Bay Area Video Coalition, 2003).

9 Chris Johanson, email to Dina Pugh, April 5, 2006.

10 In the late 1940s, scientist/philosopher Buckminster Fuller conceived of the geodesic dome based on principles of "synergetics," building on his two-decade quest to improve the housing of humanity. He predicted the housing and environmental crises that we see today and thought of the geodesic dome as a cheap, energy-efficient solution.

11 Chris Johanson, email to Dina Pugh, April 5, 2006.

12 Barry McGee. *Barry McGee*. Interview with Raphaela Platow at the artist's home-studio in the Mission District of San Francisco, March 29, 2004. Published on the occasion of an exhibition held April 29–July 25, 2004, at the Rose Art Museum of Brandeis University, unpaginated.

13 Ibid.

14 Craig Garrett, "Art and Artlessness: The Emergence of the Professional Naïve," *Flash Art* 36, no. 230 (May/June 2003), 132.

15 Nayland Blake, "Barry McGee," *Interview* (February 1999), http://www.findarticles.com/p/articles/mi_m1285/is_2_29/ai_53747378.

16 Barry McGee, "Barry McGee and Margaret Kilgallen," *Art21: Art in the Twenty-First Century*, vol. 1 (Alexandria, VA: PBS Home Video, 2001).

17 Barry McGee, *Barry McGee*. Published on the occasion of an exhibition held April 29–July 25, 2004, at the Rose Art Museum of Brandeis University, unpaginated.

18 Julian Myers, "Alicia McCarthy," *Frieze* 78 (October 2003).

19 The exceptions being the previously mentioned show at Jack Hanley, *Widely Unknown* at Deitch Projects (2001), and a solo show at RARE Gallery in New York (2002) where she once again included a piece by Sara Thustra.

20 Jo Jackson, interview by Dina Pugh, March 17, 2006.

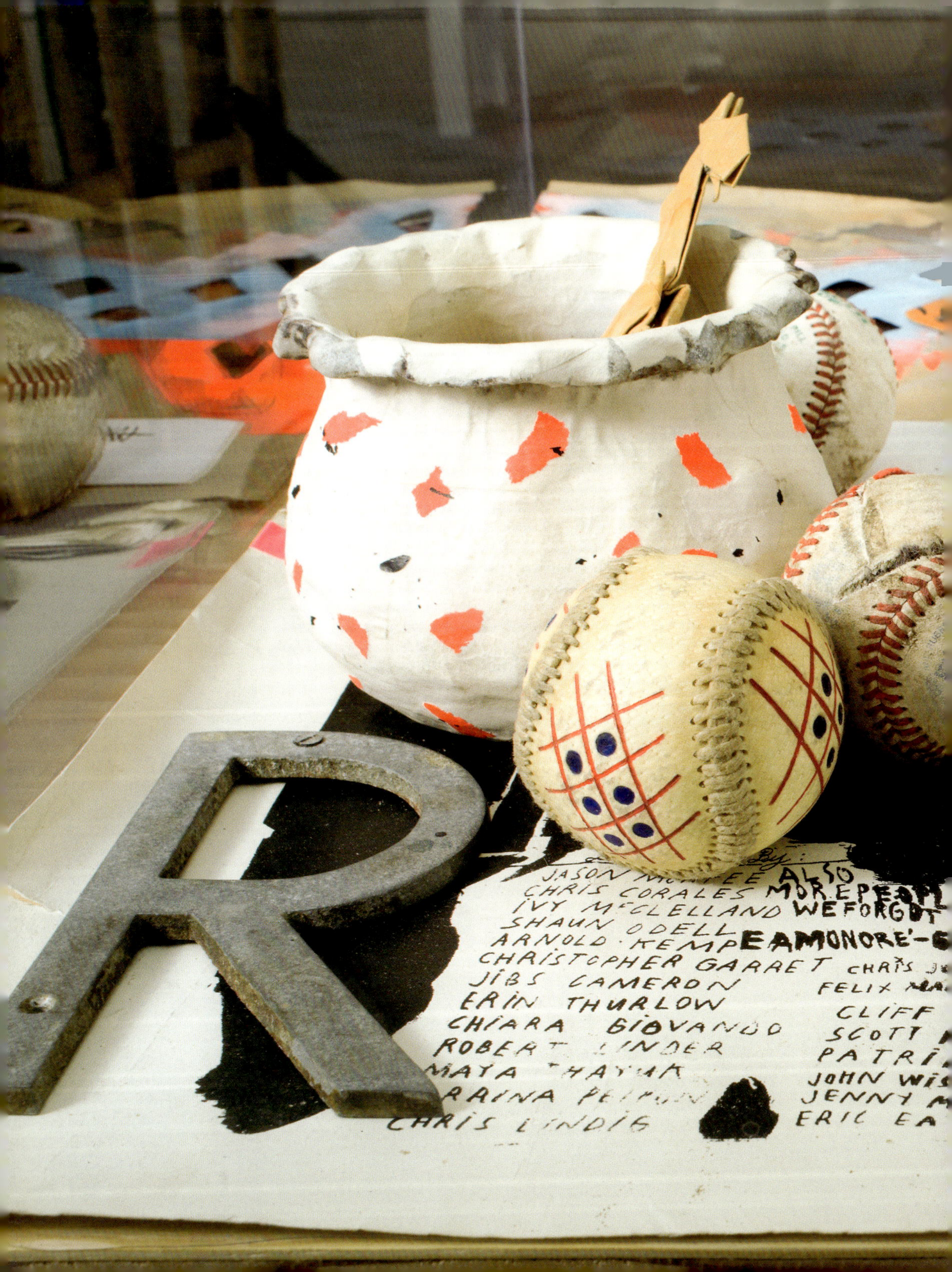
By:
ALSO
CHRIS CORALES
IVY McCLELLAND
WE FORGOT
SHAUN ODELL
ARNOLD KEMP
CHRISTOPHER GARRET
JIBS CAMERON
FELIX
ERIN THURLOW
CLIFF
CHIARA GIOVANDO
SCOTT
PATRI
JOHN WIS
JENNY
CHRIS LINDIG
ERIC EA

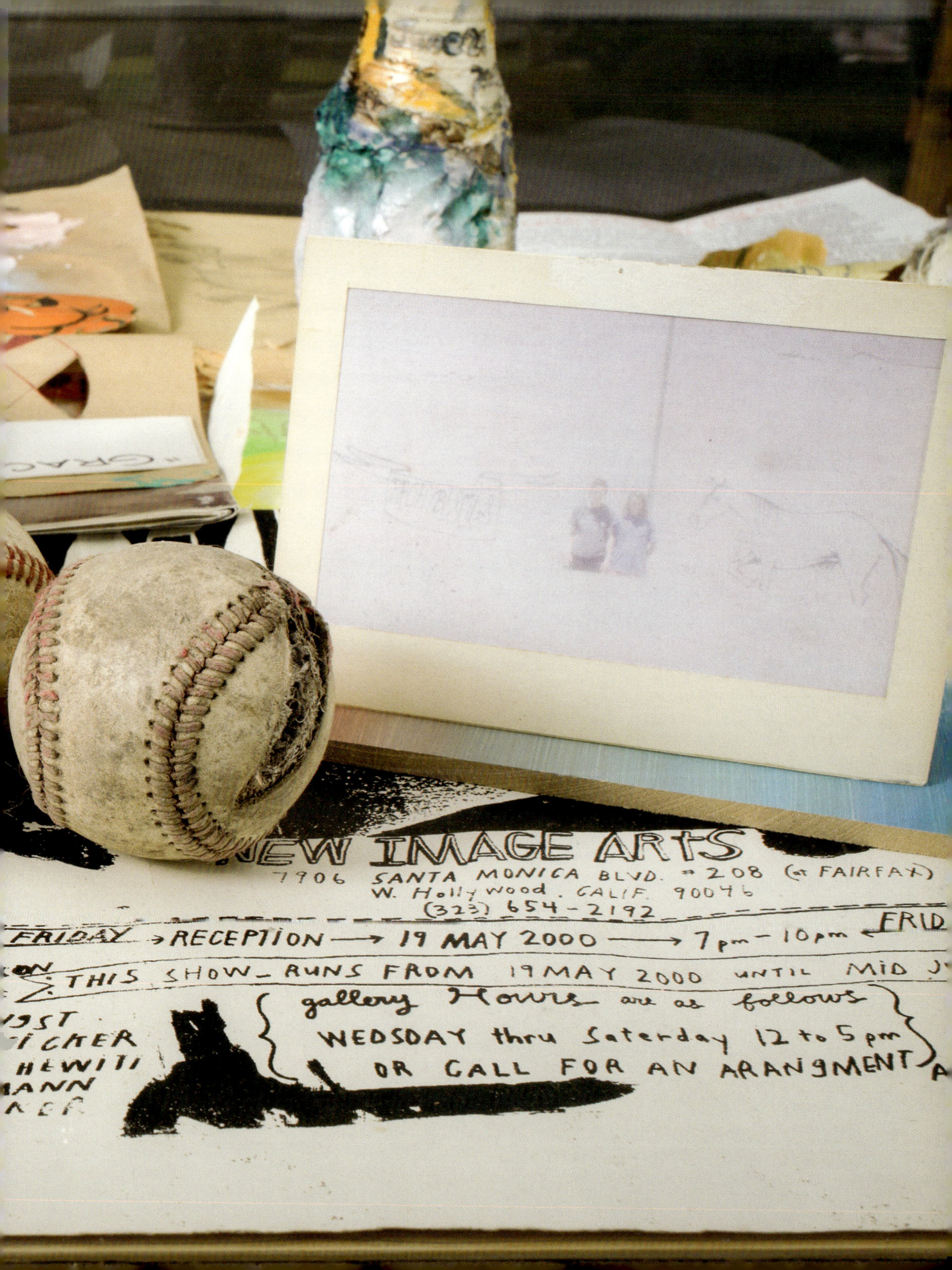
NEW IMAGE ArtS
7906 SANTA MONICA BLVD. #208 (at FAIRFAX)
W. Hollywood. CALIF. 90046
(323) 654-2192
FRIDAY → RECEPTION → 19 MAY 2000 → 7pm – 10pm
THIS SHOW_RUNS FROM 19MAY 2000 UNTIL
gallery Hours are as follows
WEDSDAY thru Saterday 12 to 5pm
OR CALL FOR AN ARANGMENT

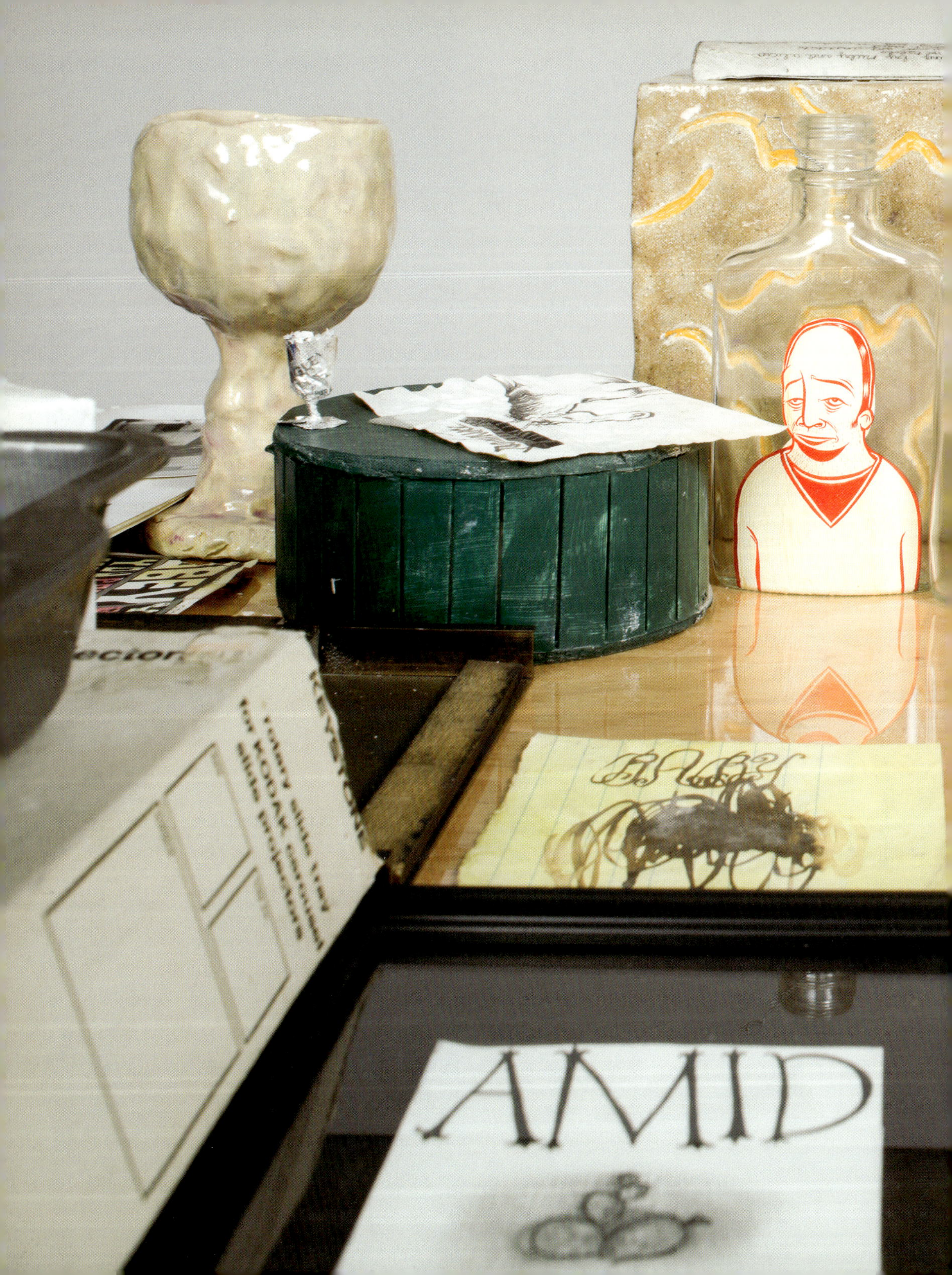
AMID

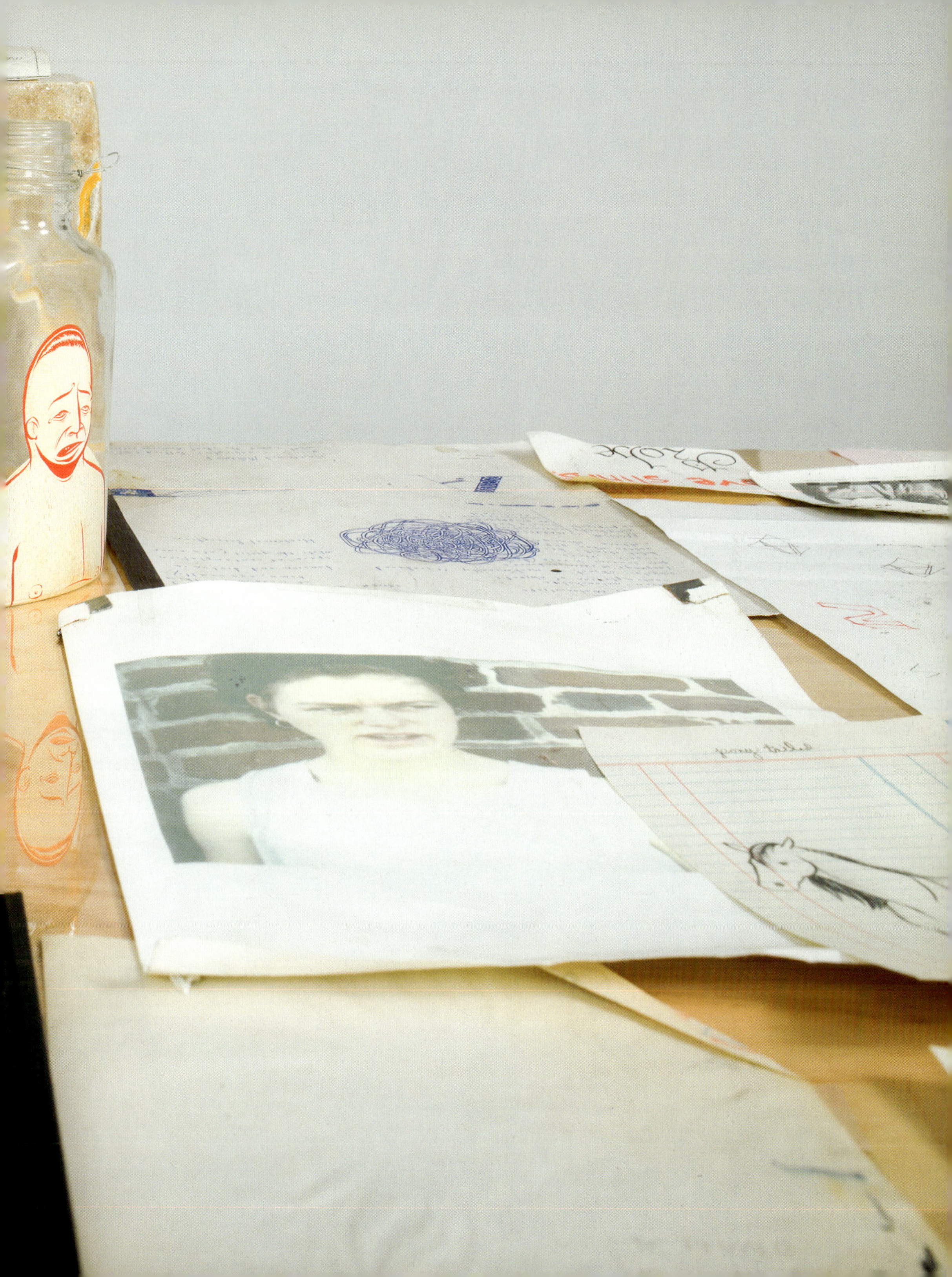
pony tailed

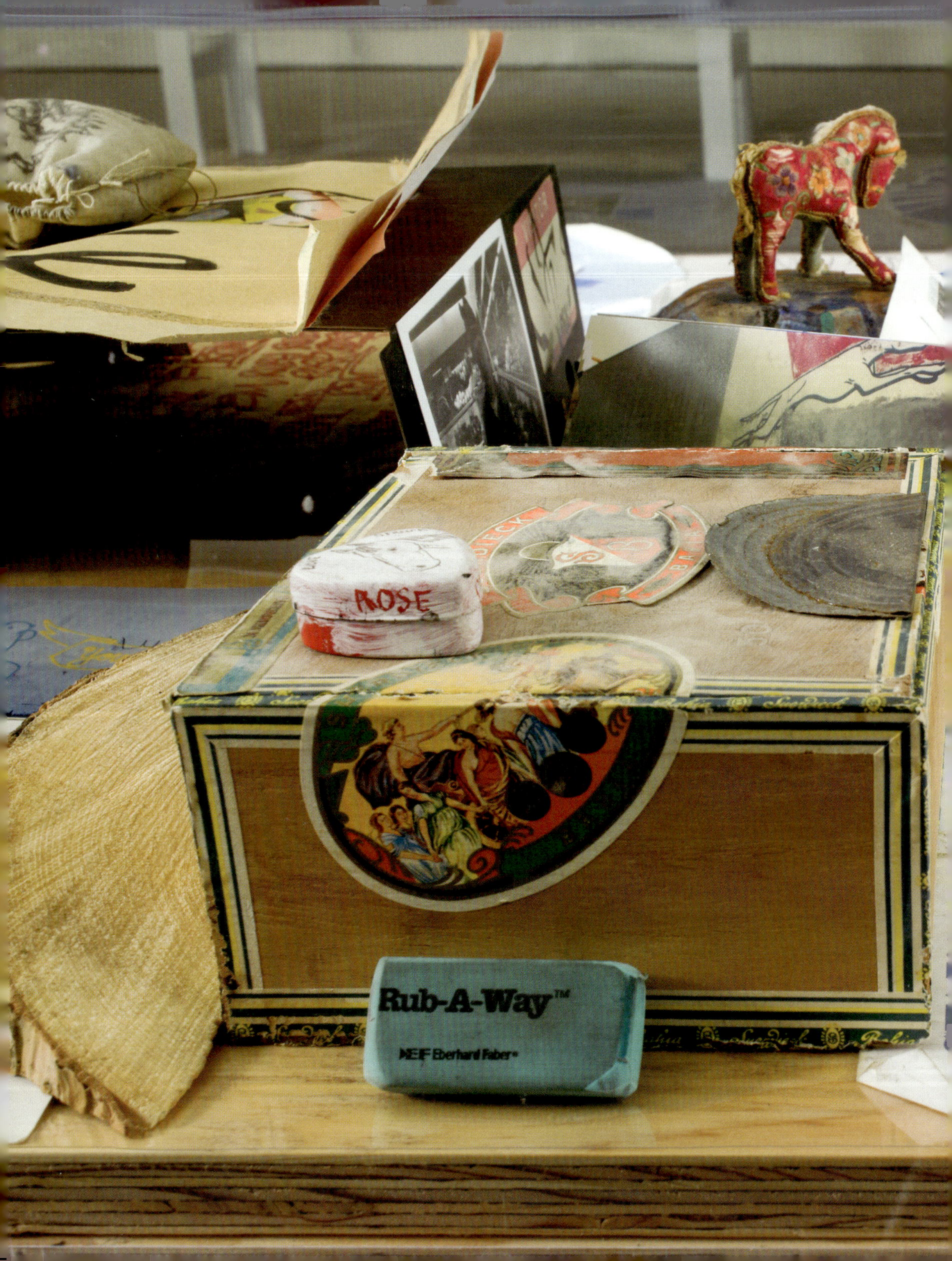
ROSE
Rub-A-Way™
Eberhard Faber

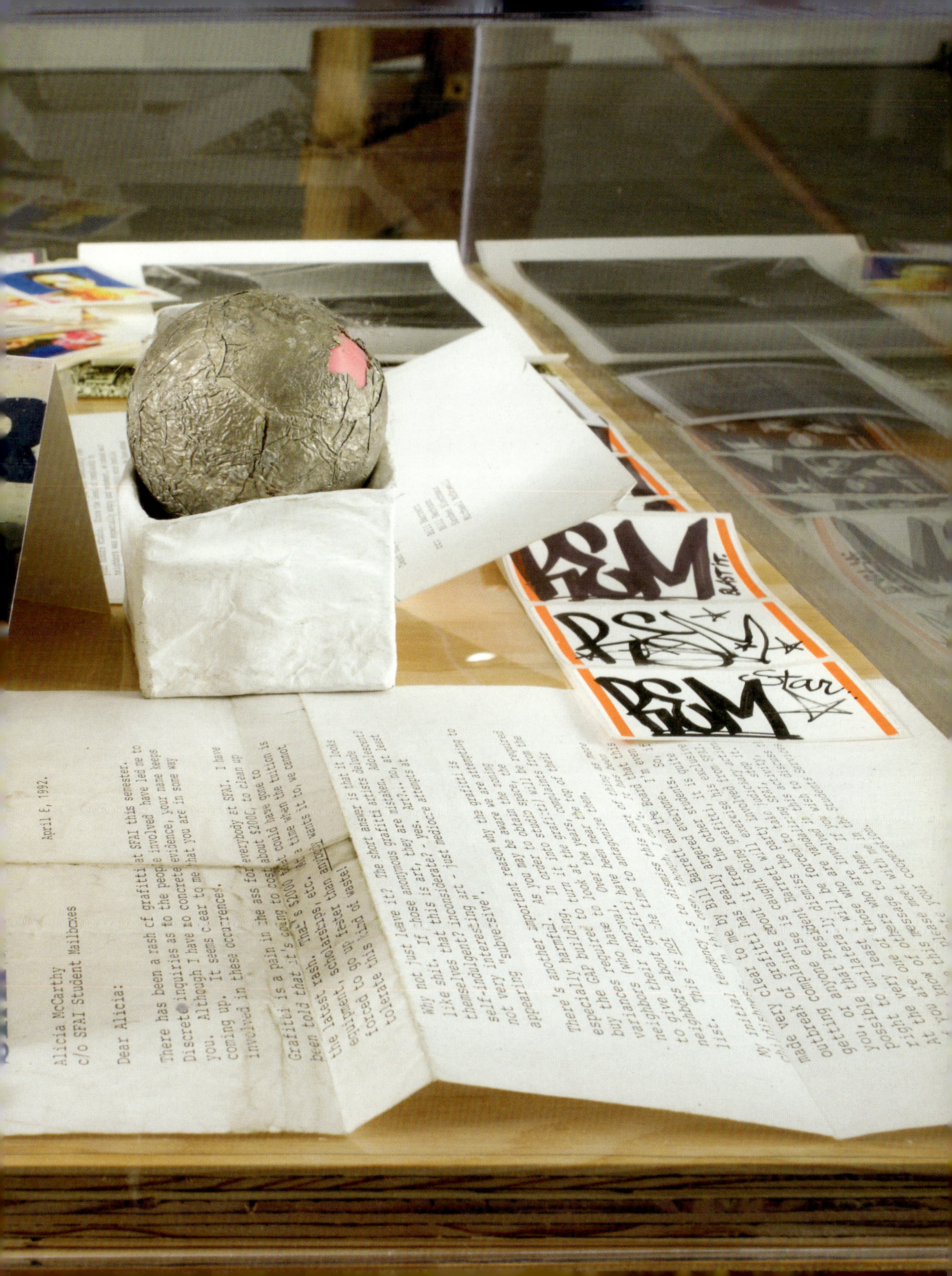
April 6, 1992.
Alicia McCarthy
c/o SFAI Student Mailboxes
Dear Alicia:

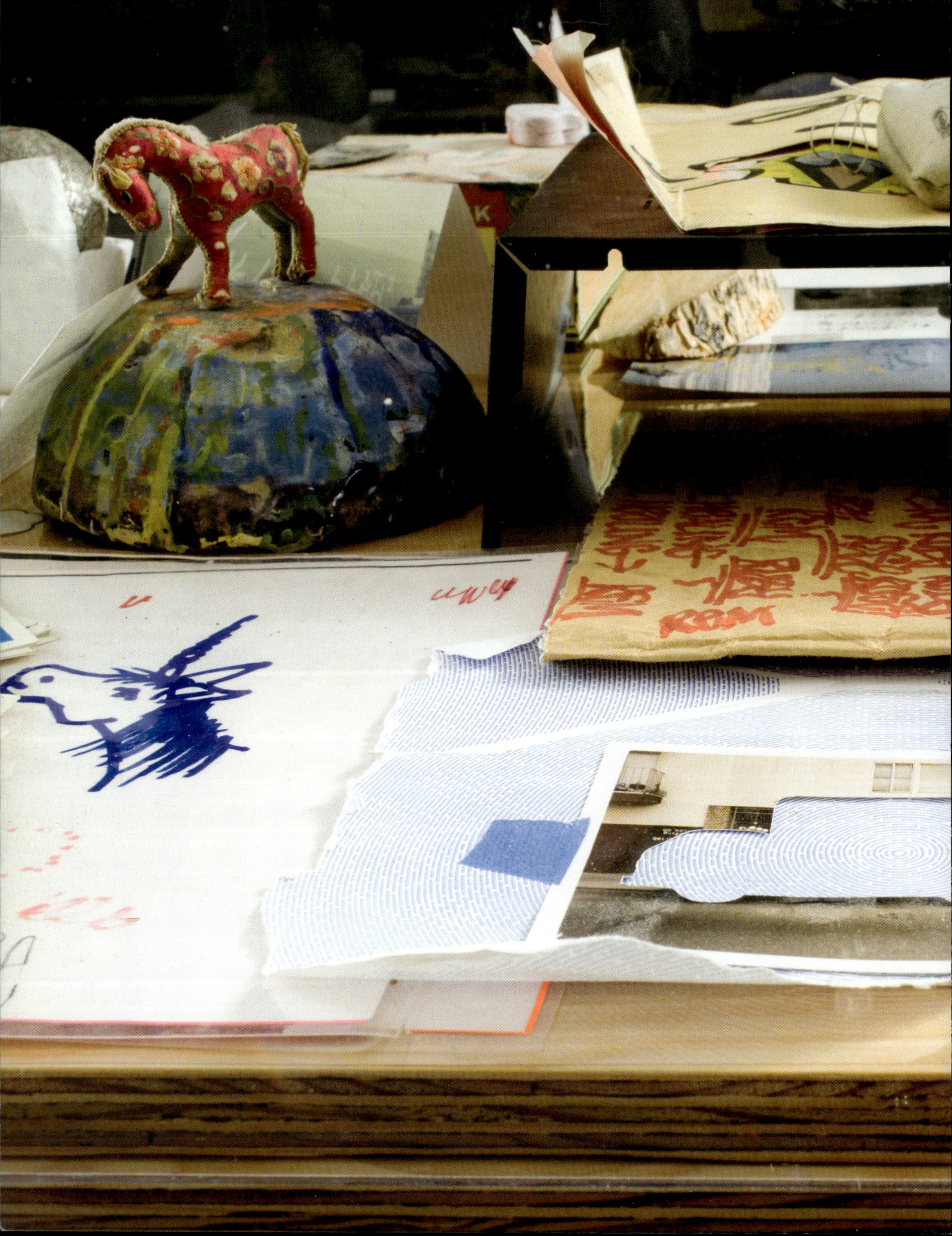

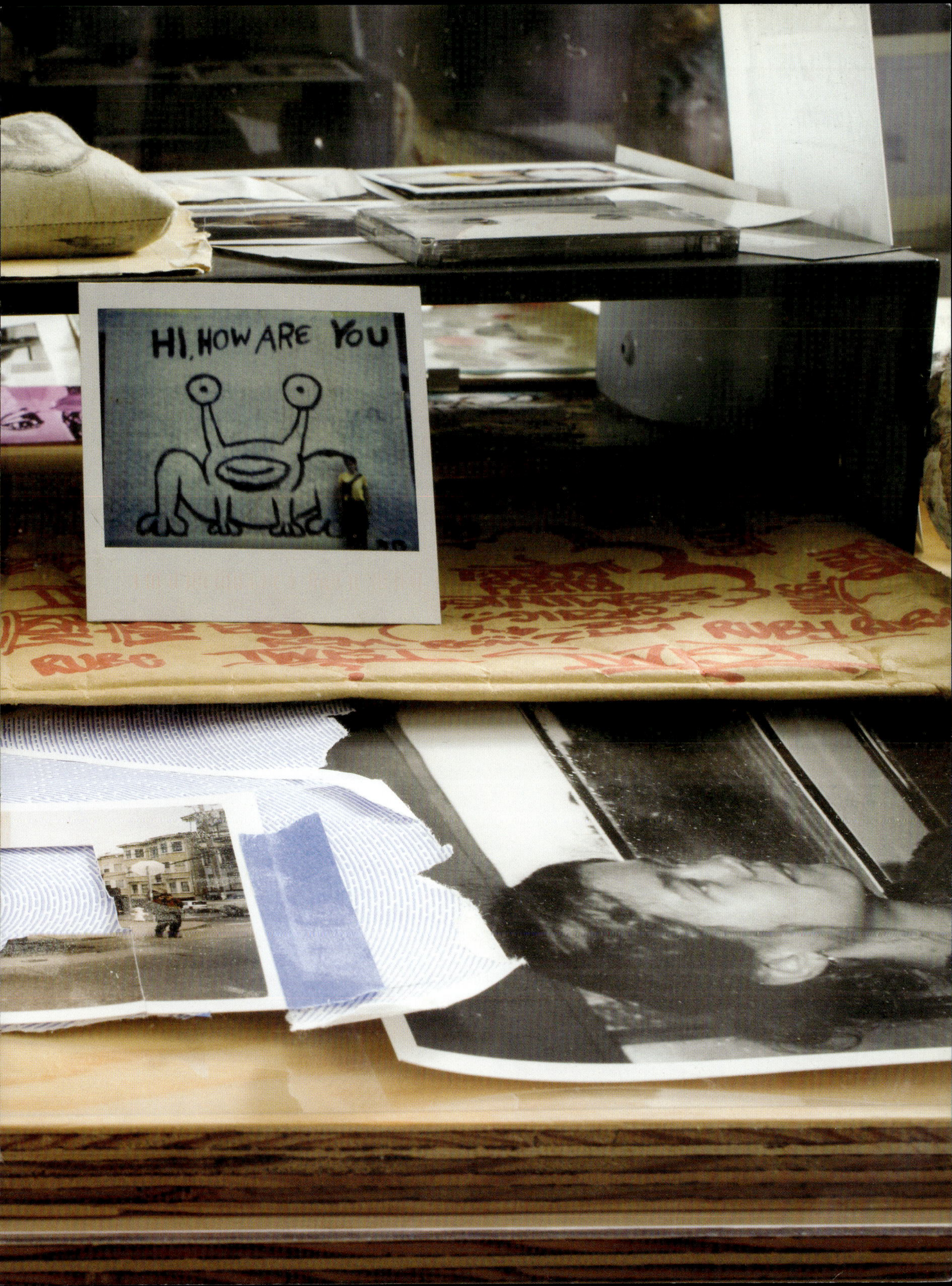
HI, HOW ARE YOU

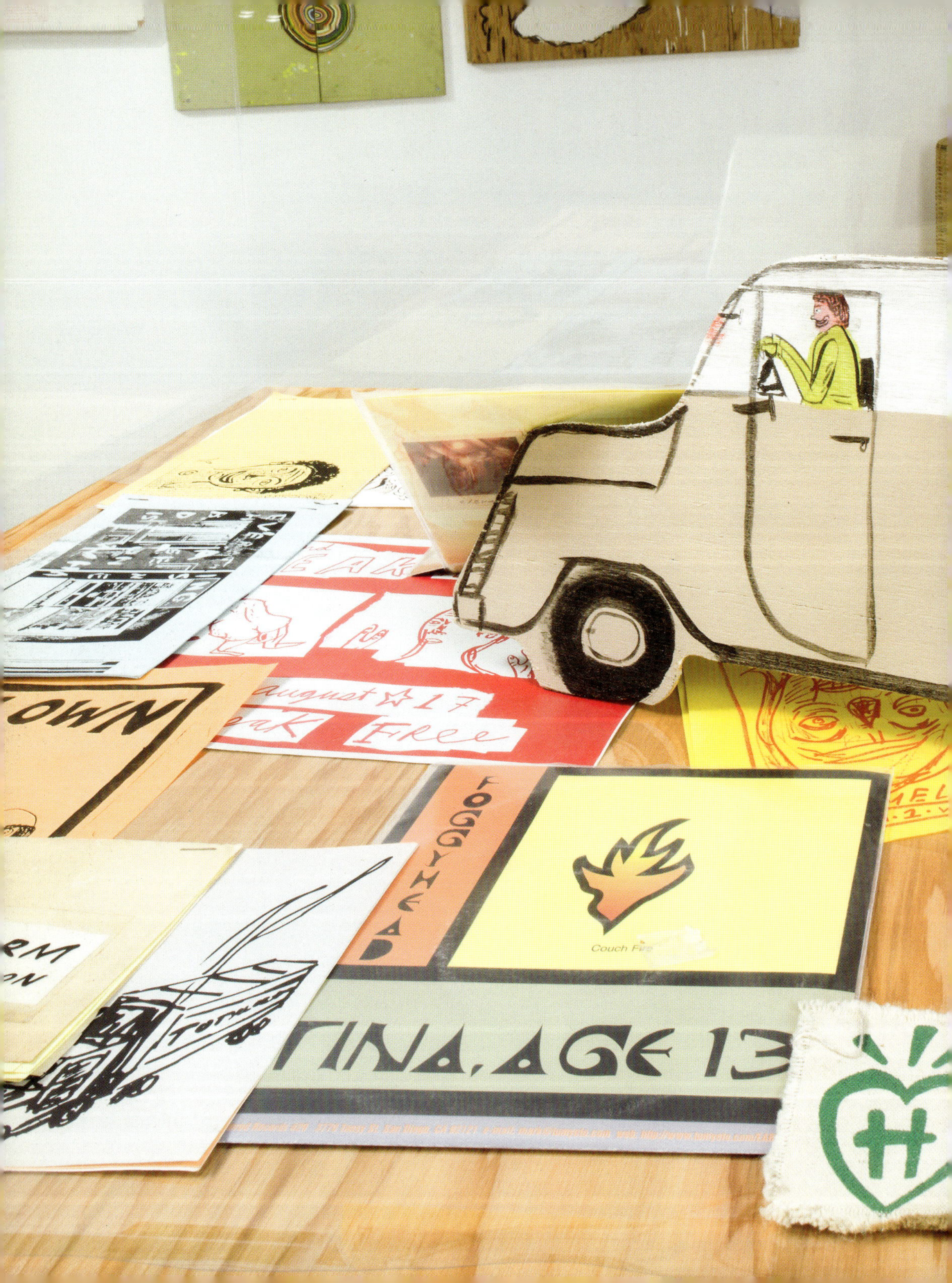
FOGGYHEAD
TINA, AGE 13
august☆17

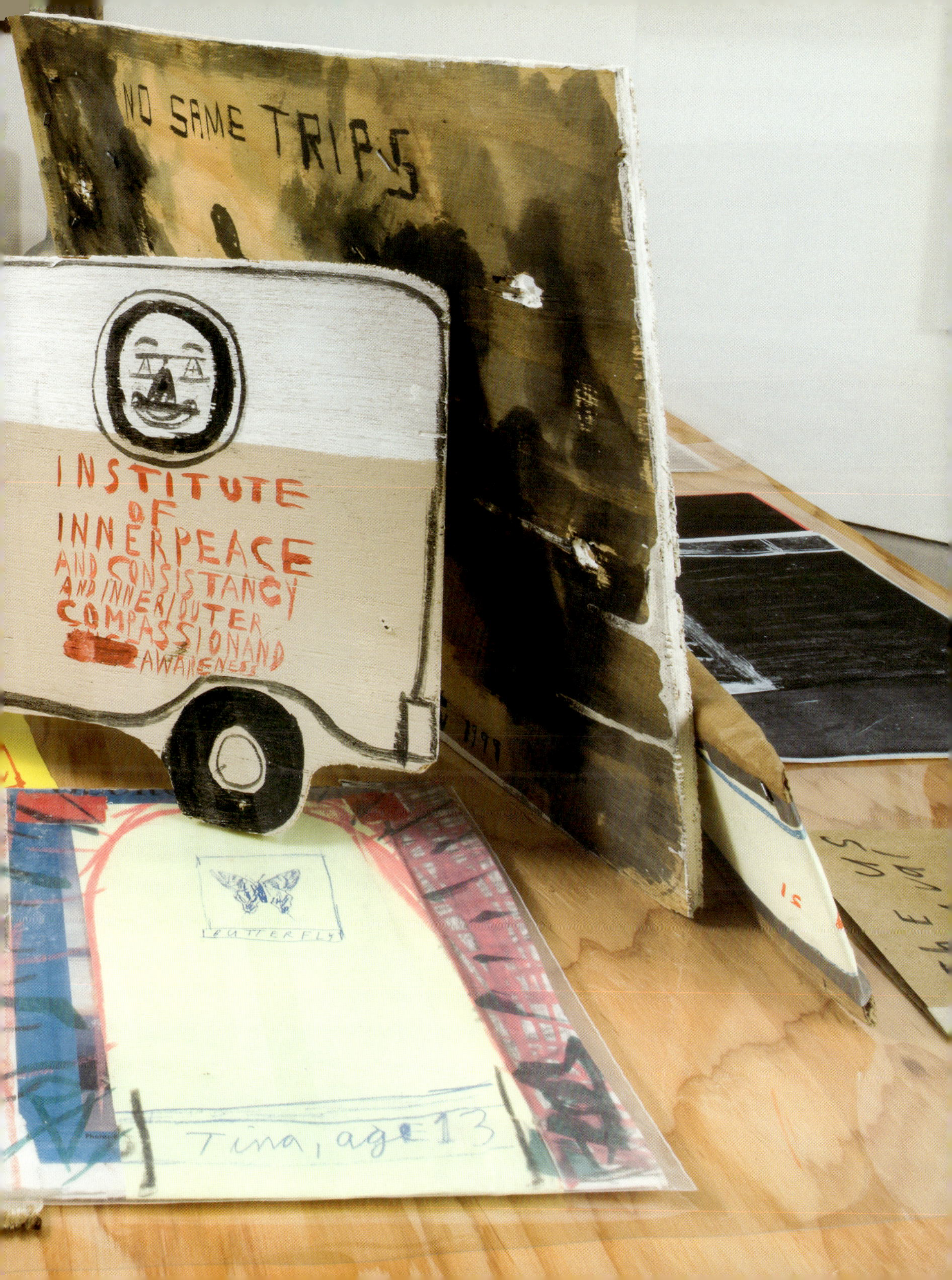
NO SAME TRIPS
INSTITUTE OF INNERPEACE AND CONSISTANCY AND INNER/OUTER COMPASSIONAND
AWARENESS
BUTTERFLY
Tina, age 13

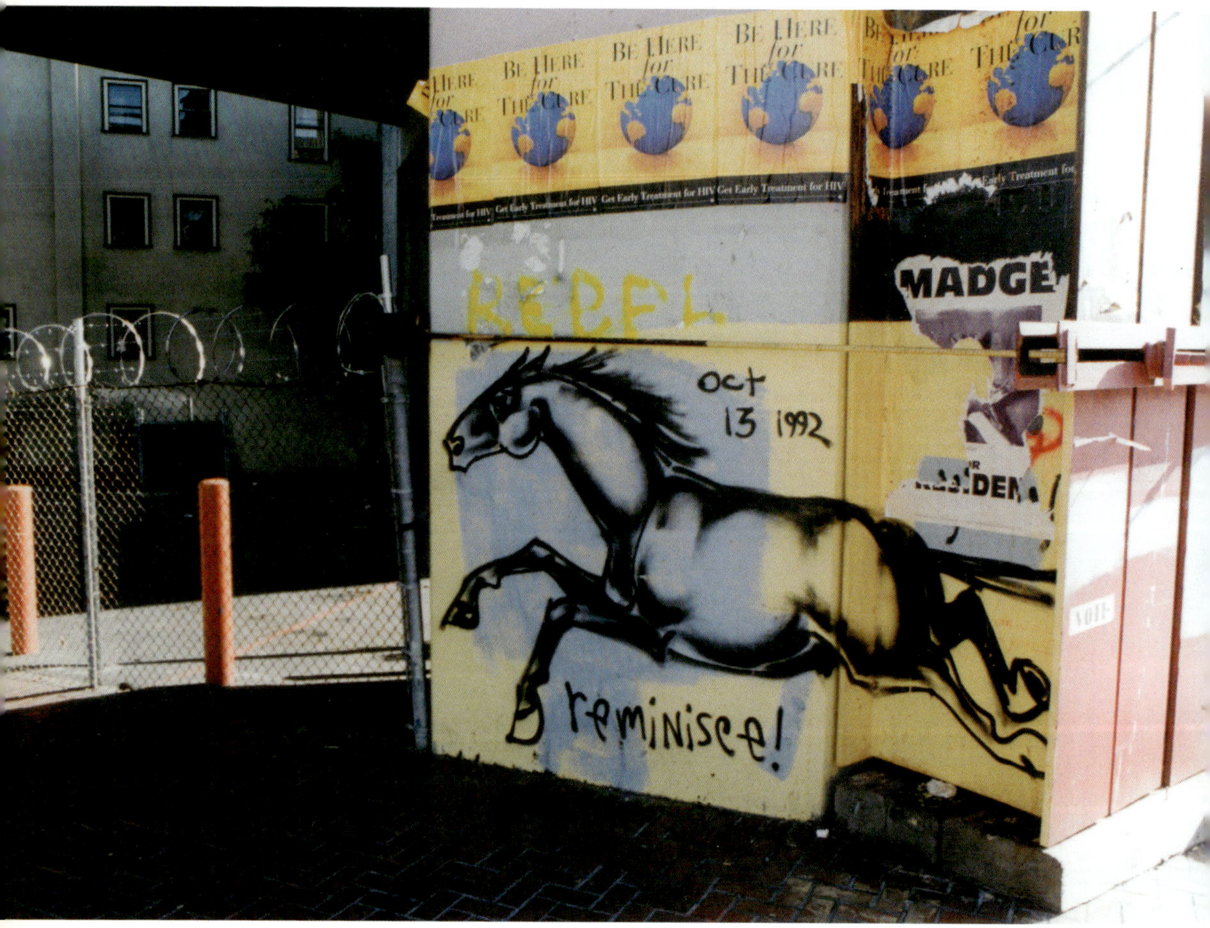
BE HERE for THE CURE
Get Early Treatment for HIV
MADGE
oct 13 1992
reminisce!

THE MISSION SCHOOL

San Francisco's Street Artists Deliver Their Neighborhood to the Art World

BY GLEN HELFAND

Excerpts from an article originally published July 1, 2002, in the San Francisco Bay Guardian

IF PLACES LIKE THE LEFT BANK and Greenwich Village feel vaguely *historical*, it's pleasing to note that artistic movements, even under the reign of globalism, can still be traced to neighborhoods, the physical places where artists, writers, and thinkers congregate. Perhaps because San Francisco is so compact, its cultural innovations, more than many other cities', have always been identified with specific, romanticized intersections. Castro and Market, gay liberation. Haight and Ashbury, hippies. Columbus and Broadway, Beats. Most recently, 16th Street and Mission has become the locus of a yet to be labeled brand of art that's become one of San Francisco's most notable exports.

In the art world, however, the idea of provincialism is viewed with suspicion and even condescension, which is why it's somehow so satisfying that Barry McGee, Margaret Kilgallen—who succumbed to cancer last year at 33—and Chris Johanson, among others, have become international icons of a thirtysomething generation of San Francisco artists who mine an aesthetic of the local streets. For them, it's a road that, surprisingly, has led to huge

RUBY NERI
Reminisce graffiti, 1992

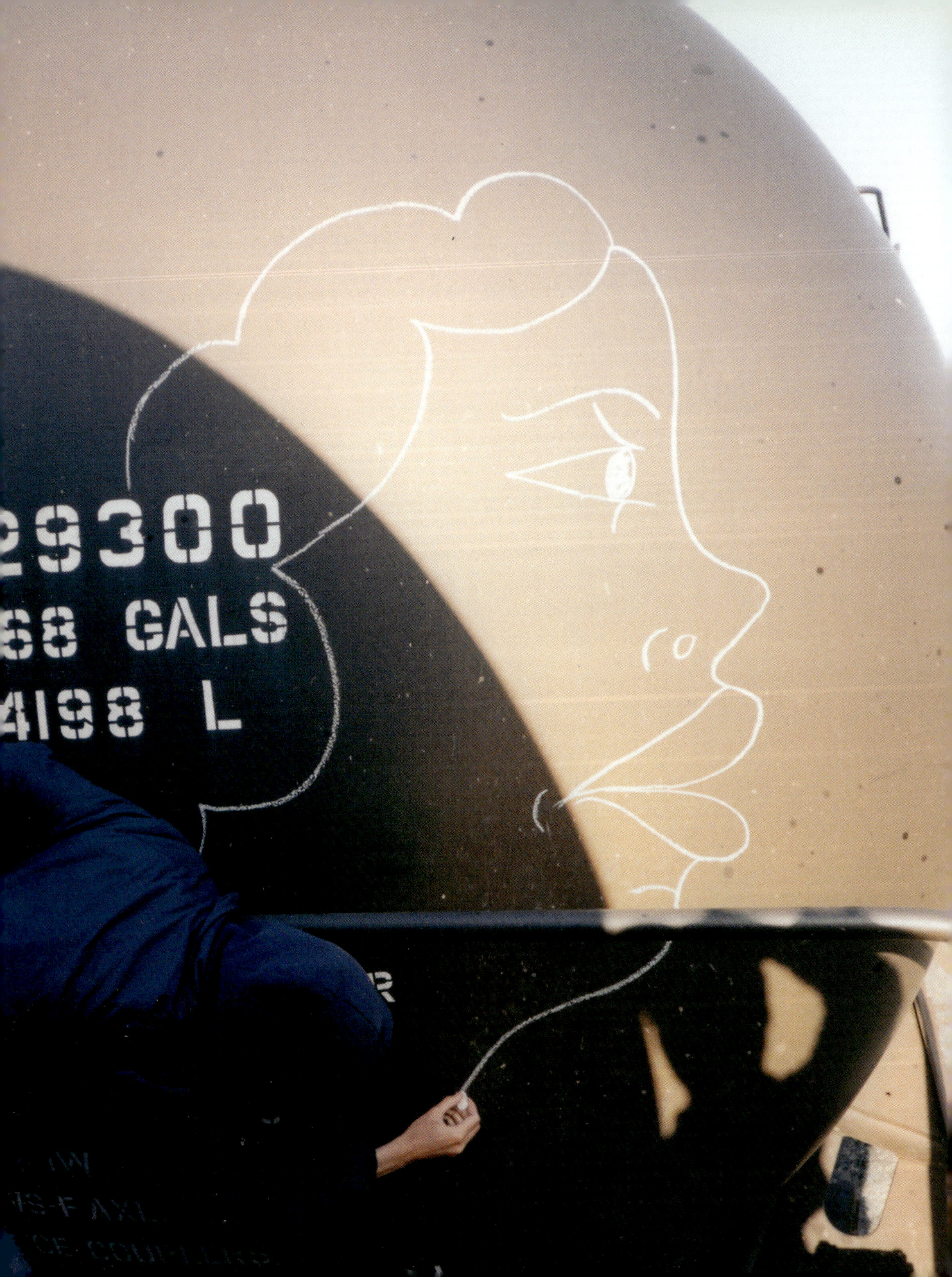
29300
68 GALS
4198 L

popularity in New York and even Japan, illustrating the old rock and roll truism that sometimes an artist has to leave the country to get real notice at home.

It's even more satisfying that these artists have gone global with an extremely humane and honest approach. Their work is heartfelt, handmade, and deeply observational, and its urban realism is filtered through interests in graffiti, comic books, green culture, and social activism. They're refreshingly scrappy, modest, hardworking, and community oriented, attributes that resonate in a climate of global uncertainty and palpable physical threat. They serve as an indigenous piece of the Bay Area's art history in the unstudied way they incorporate the experiential drive of Bay Area conceptualism (see Tom Marioni's 1970 *The Act of Drinking Beer with Friends Is the Highest Form of Art*), the revered Bay Area Figurative School, and perhaps a gentle counterbalance to the scarier politicized street robotics of Survival Research Laboratories.

While the funky, assured projects the current generation of artists creates may not suit everyone's tastes—this is material rooted more in an "up with people" spirit, and sometimes a messy, childlike ethos, than in the shiny, distanced intellectual aura of art theory and media critique that informs much other contemporary art—no one can argue the fact that the generous neighborhood spirit of their work is appealing. Whether it's "Think globally, act locally," or the same process in reverse, there's a certain bumper-sticker enthusiasm to this ad hoc artistic movement, which is being called everything from "urban rustic" to "The Mission school." . . .

INSIDE/OUTSIDE WORLD

San Francisco's position as a more casual art market than New York, Los Angeles, or Chicago allows for just that kind of pondering. It permits many to sidestep the distractions of competitive art-world climbing, though this low-pressure condition is the very thing that causes a large number of promising artists to head to those bigger

Margaret Kilgallen, ca. 1998

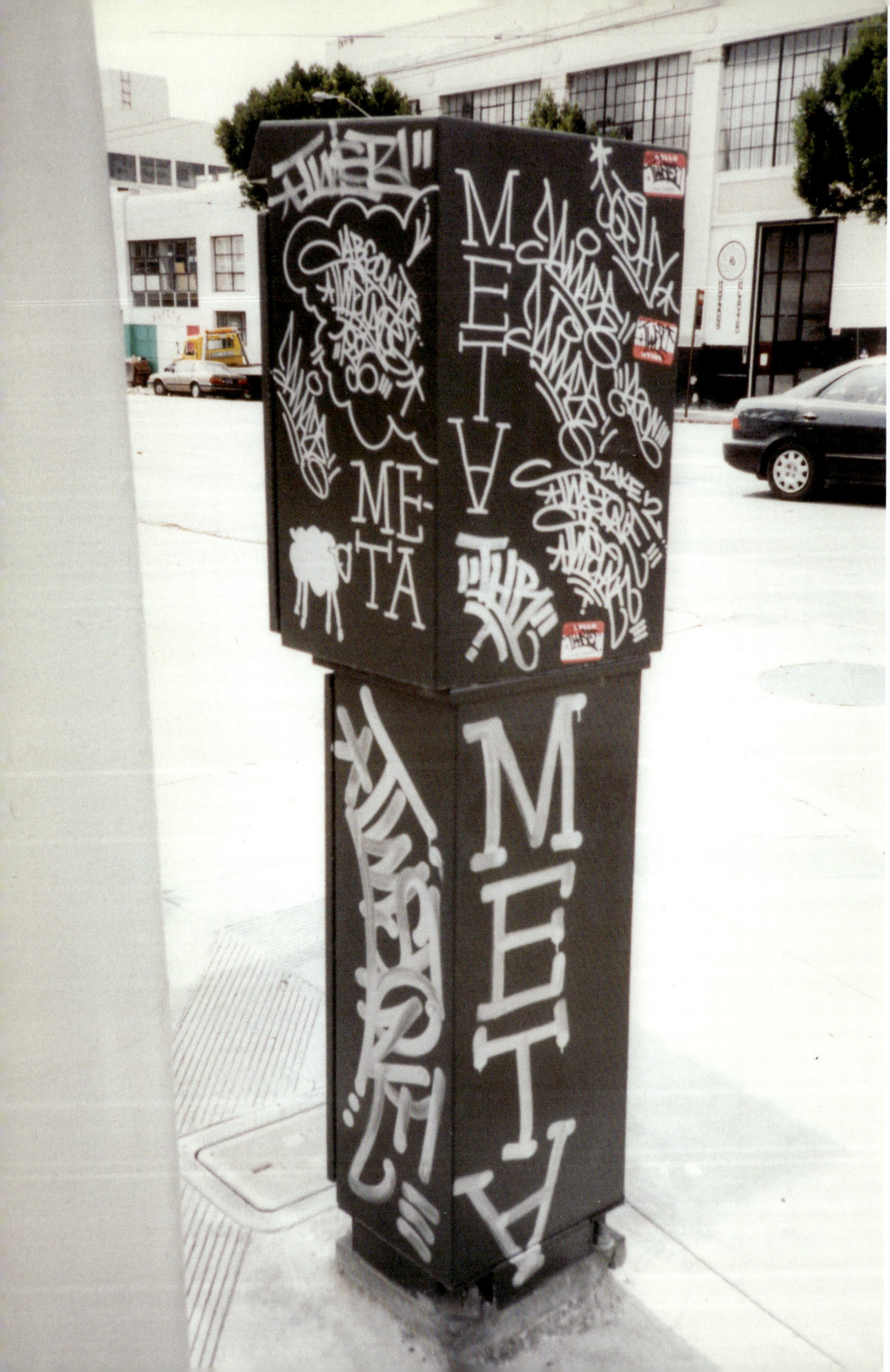
META
ME-
TA
TAKE 2
META

centers to forge a career after honing their craft and ideas here. The fact that this particular crop of artists can use San Francisco as a base, tapping into its various grassroots energies, yet create projects internationally is a hopeful sign. . . .

BRAND: NEW

The mythic narrative of the street adds appeal to the tales of these artists. This isn't a calculated effort, however. Rather, it's the natural outgrowth of talented people working in the same area, having a dialogue. Since we live in a brand-driven world, though, it's not surprising that a group of like-minded artists' work would generate a brand name that's easily adaptable to Bay Area art history, not to mention the marketplace.

"When you look back at the Beat scene, that was less than a 10-year period," says Ed Gilbert, director of Gallery Paule Anglim, which will show McGee's work this May. "And there were distinct relationships between the key figures. There's something similar about the current group of artists who emerged when the SoMa, graffiti, and skateboard scenes were intersecting with art-educated kids. Down the road, they might be simplified into a bit of history."

Buzz terms have been cropping up. *The Mission school* has been uttered with some regularity. *Urban Rustics* and *Digital Bohemians* were the terms given in an article by Yerba Buena Center for the Arts curator Renny Pritikin. "Born between 1965 and 1975, as children and young adults they have endured corporate eco-porn advertising and the simultaneous creation of the professionalization of the environmental movement," he writes in an article to be published in a book of Amy Franceschini's work. "Their resulting cynicism about good environmental intentions and rhetoric is wed to an absolutely conflicting near-religious belief in salvaging what is left of a fugitive authentic world."

San Francisco, ca. 1998

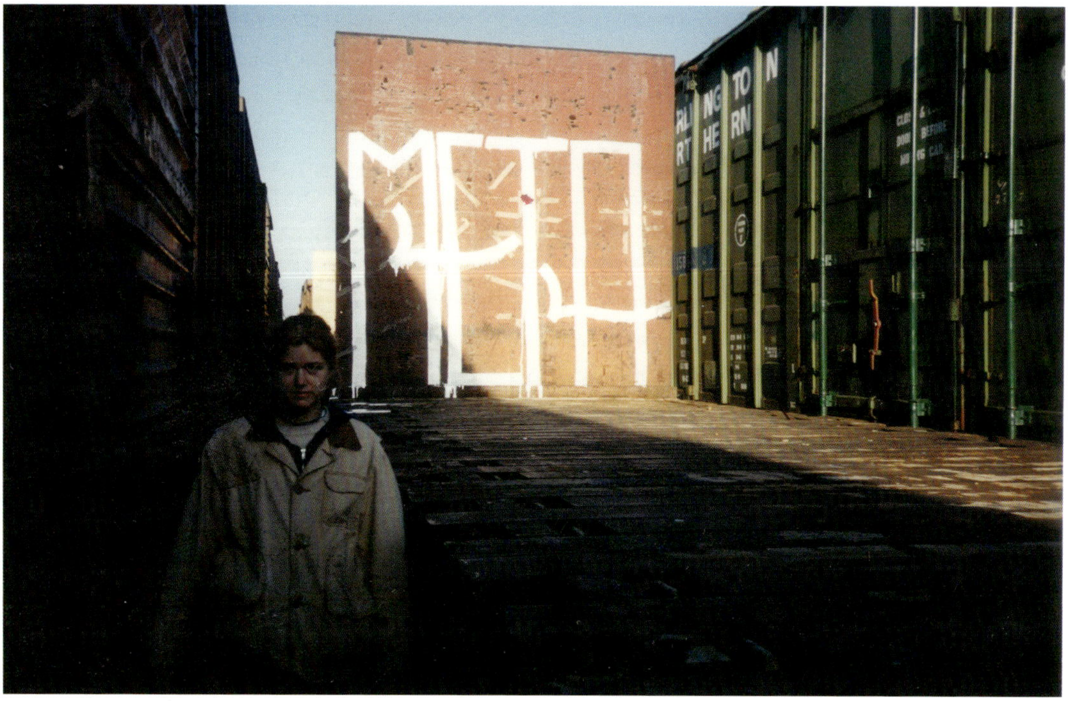

Eungie Joo, the former Bay Area writer and curator who organized *Widely Unknown*, terms this work "the new folk" in a forthcoming article in the international art magazine *Flash Art*. "A new wave of work that actively defies distinction between high and low art forms and demonstrates an anticapitalist's sympathy and respect for the old, worn, and recycled," she writes, identifying San Francisco as a center of its production.

Joo, now based in New York, has curated a number of exhibitions around the work of McGee, Kilgallen, and their peers, most recently at the request of gallery owner Jeffrey Deitch. "He offered the opportunity to create a context for these artists, which has been lacking," she says. The large-scale New York venue has been supportive, mounting solo shows and publishing books devoted to McGee, Kilgallen, and Johanson (who will appear there later this year). "The interest in these artists, however, has been a little slow in coming," Joo continues. "Maybe it's about national exposure and what people think of the S.F. scene and its own self-proclaimed provincialism. As much as I respect what people do in the Bay Area, you have to admit it is a tiny place."

BAY AREA AESTHETIC

It may, however, be the intimate scale that allowed these artists to forge their visions. So many of them developed in small spaces like the Luggage Store, near the fragrant intersection of Market Street near 6th. "Their work exudes a sincere expression of self," says Laurie Lazar, who codirects the space with Darryl Smith. "They're not trying to impress anybody; they're passionate—qualities that have the capacity to reach a broad cross section of people." . . .

Larry Rinder, chief curator at the Whitney, who came to the position after stints at the Berkeley Art Museum and the California College of Arts and Crafts (now the Wattis Institute), clearly found something here for the Biennial, a show that's the closest the art world comes to the Oscars. "I didn't make the Bay Area selections with any preconceptions about what I wanted to represent," Rinder says. "As with art from anywhere in the country, I simply selected works that I found to be vital, urgent, and compelling. . . ."

The essay in its entirety can be accessed at www.sfbg.com/36/28/art_mission_school.html.

Margaret Kilgallen, ca. 1998

left
BARRY McGEE
UNTITLED, *1992*

right
ALICIA McCARTHY
UNTITLED, *1995*

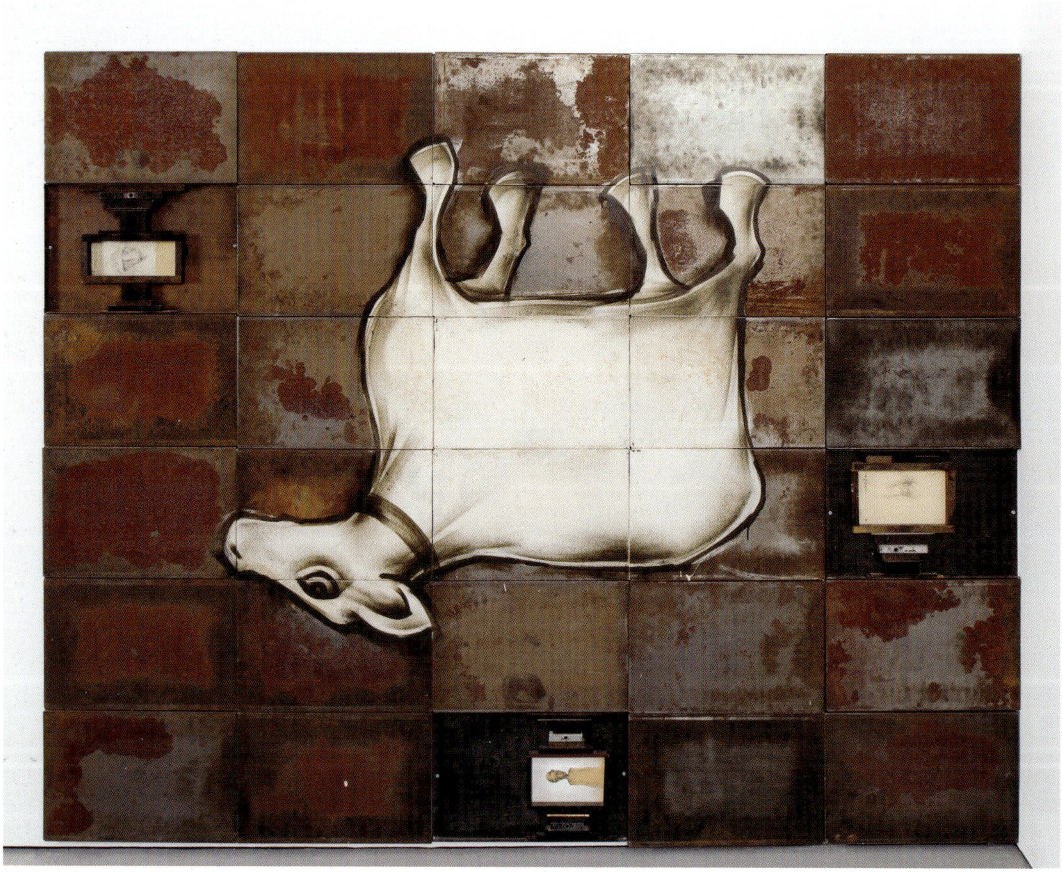

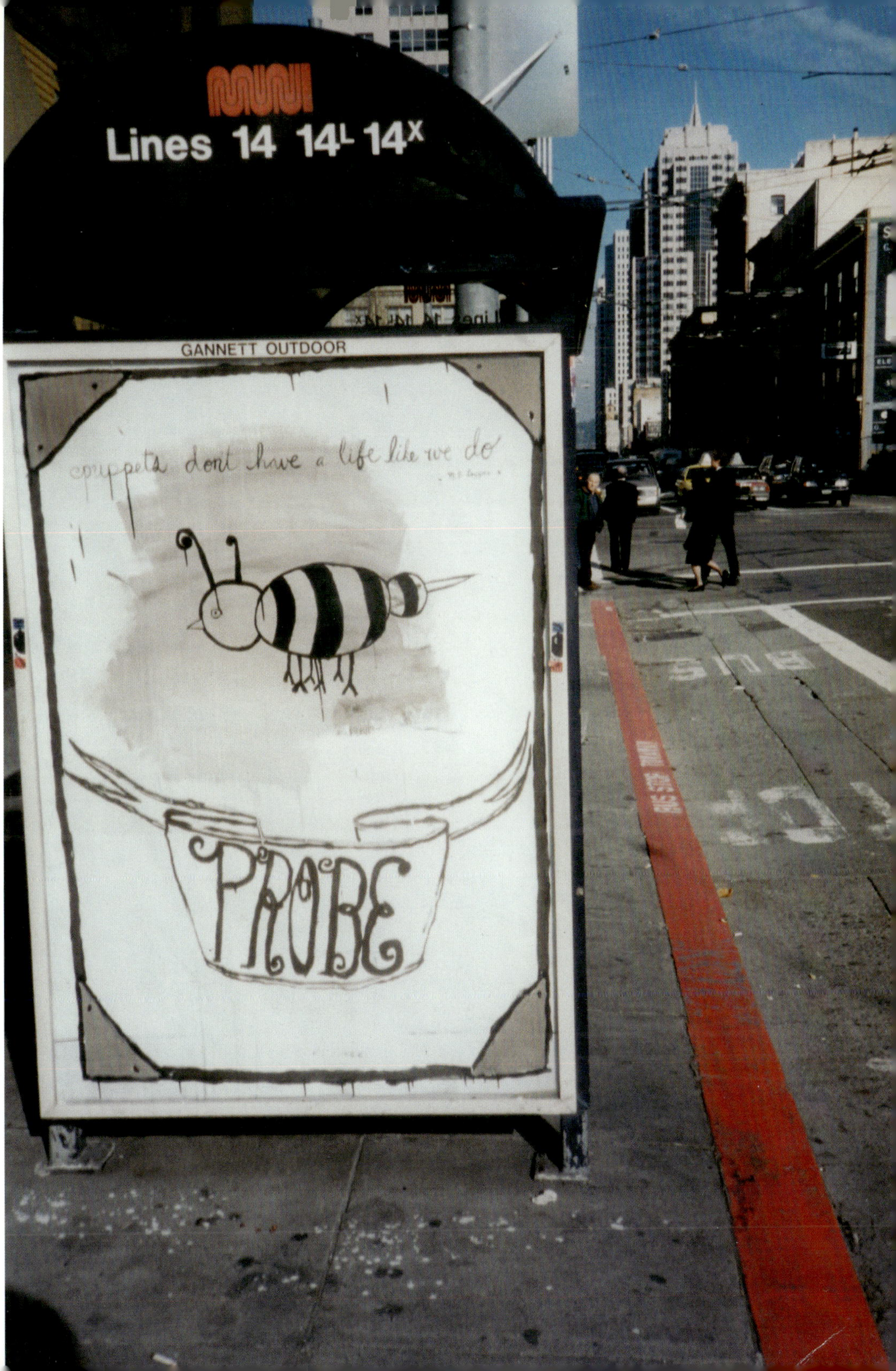
Lines 14 14L 14X
GANNETT OUTDOOR
puppets dont have a life like we do
PROBE

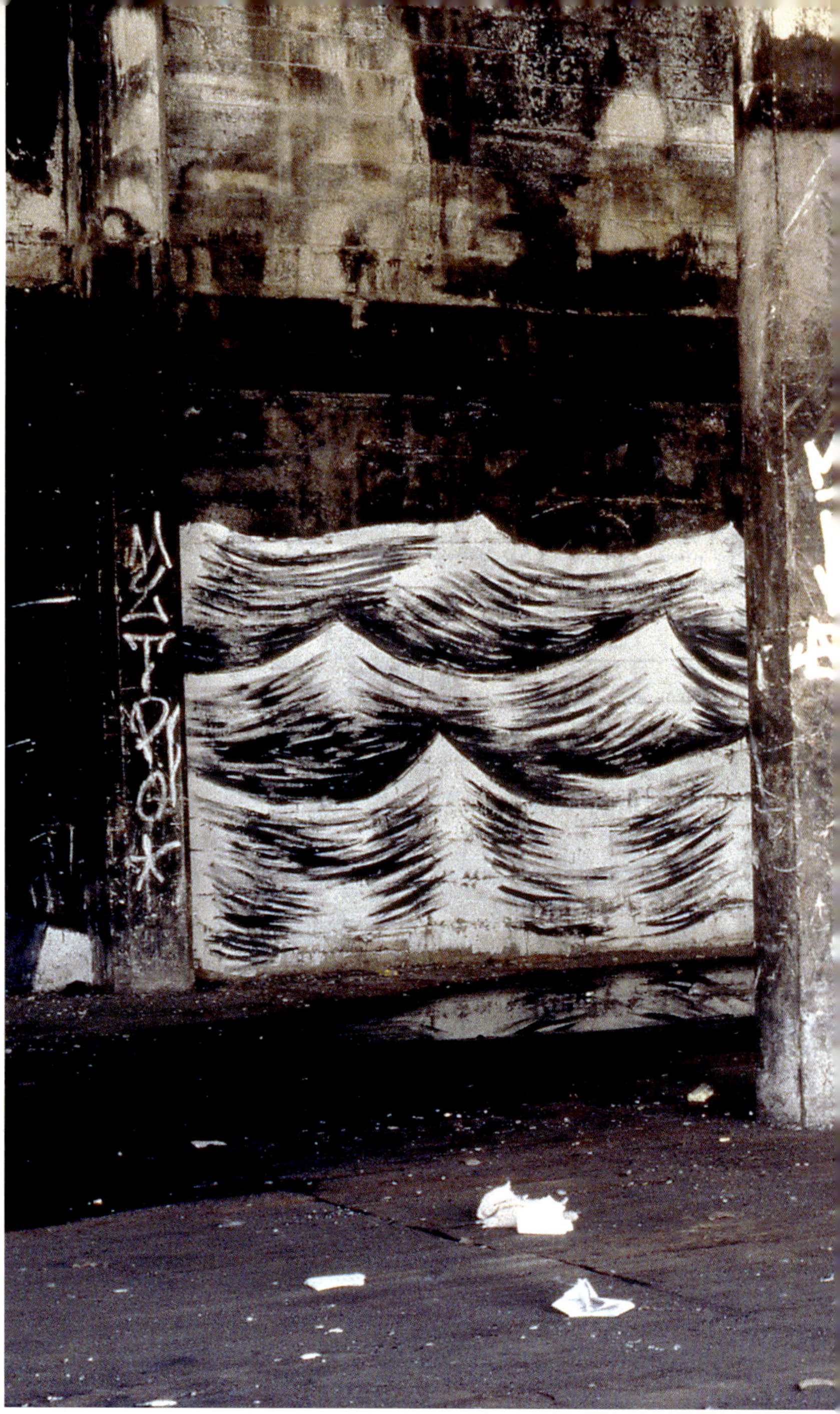

RUBY NERI
Untitled wall mural, ca. 1994

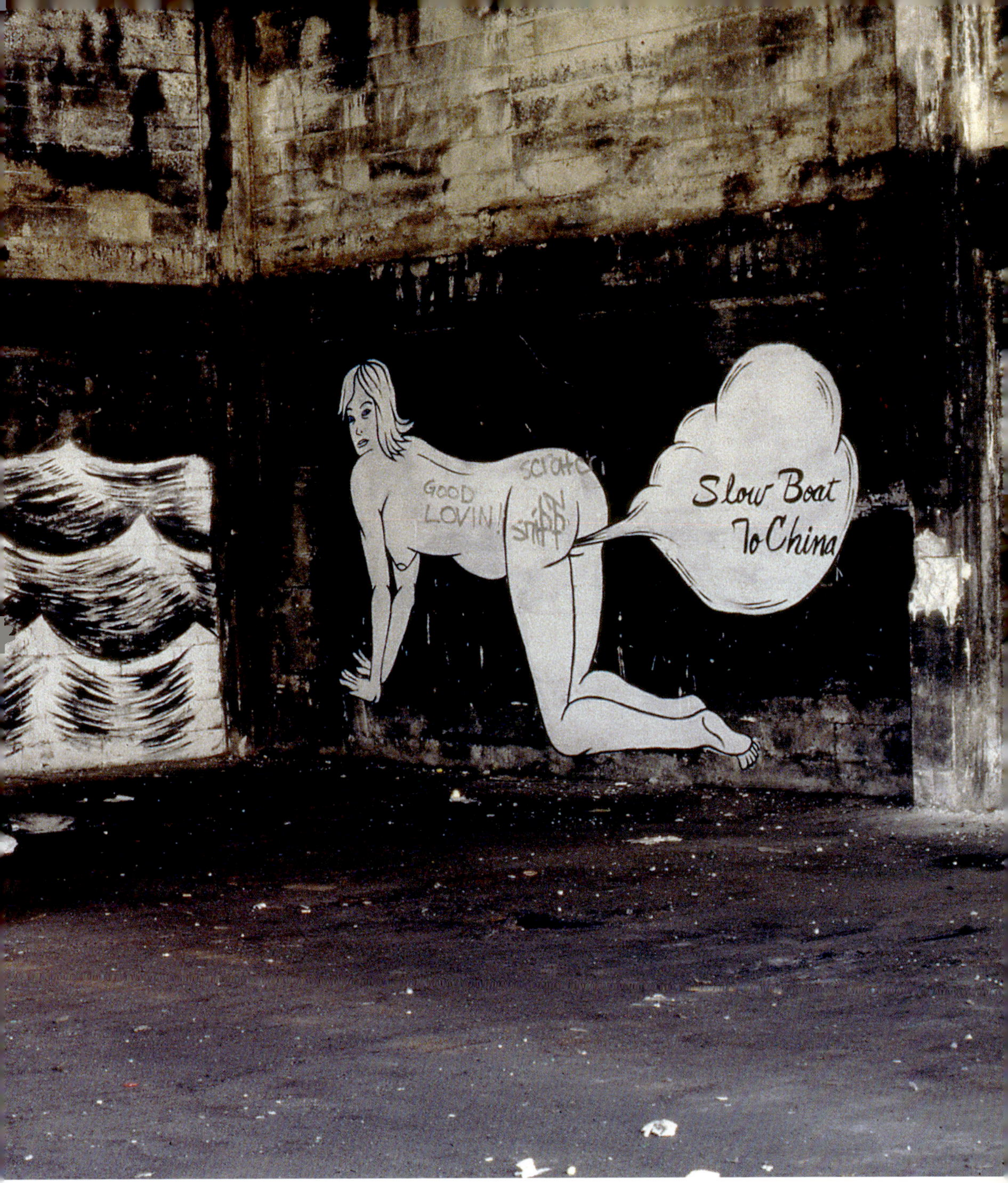
GOOD
LOVIN!
Slow Boat
To China

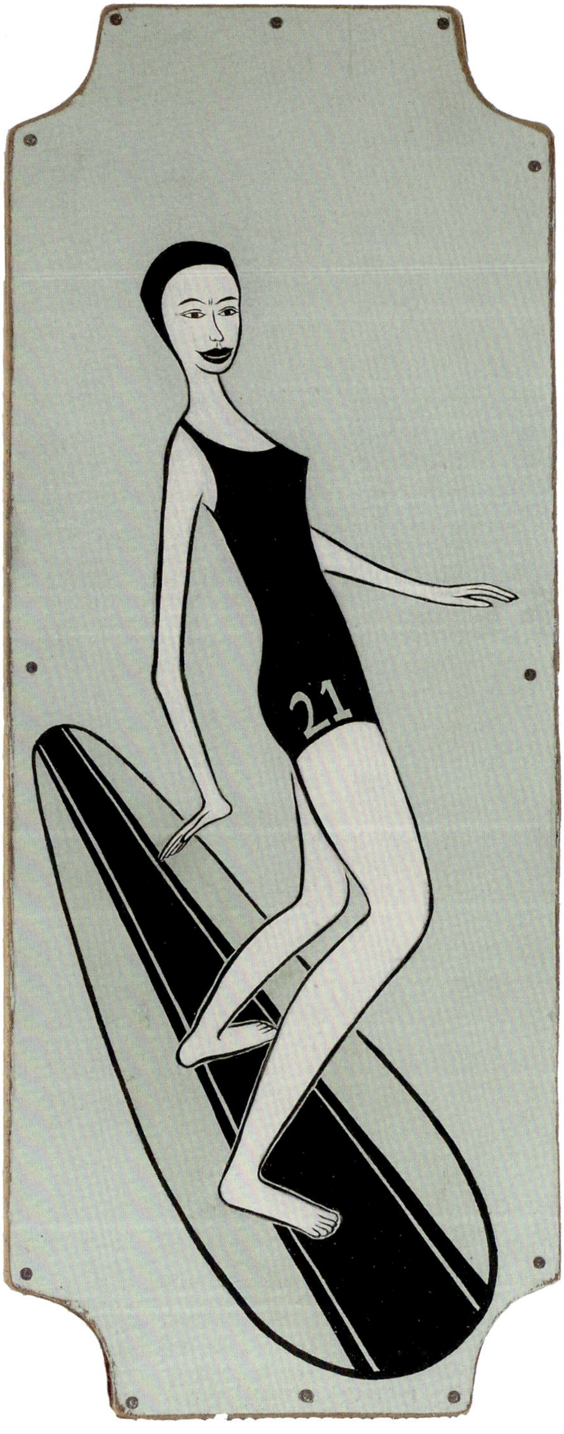

left
MARGARET KILGALLEN
SURFER GIRL, *ca. 1992*

right
BARRY McGEE
UNTITLED, *1994*

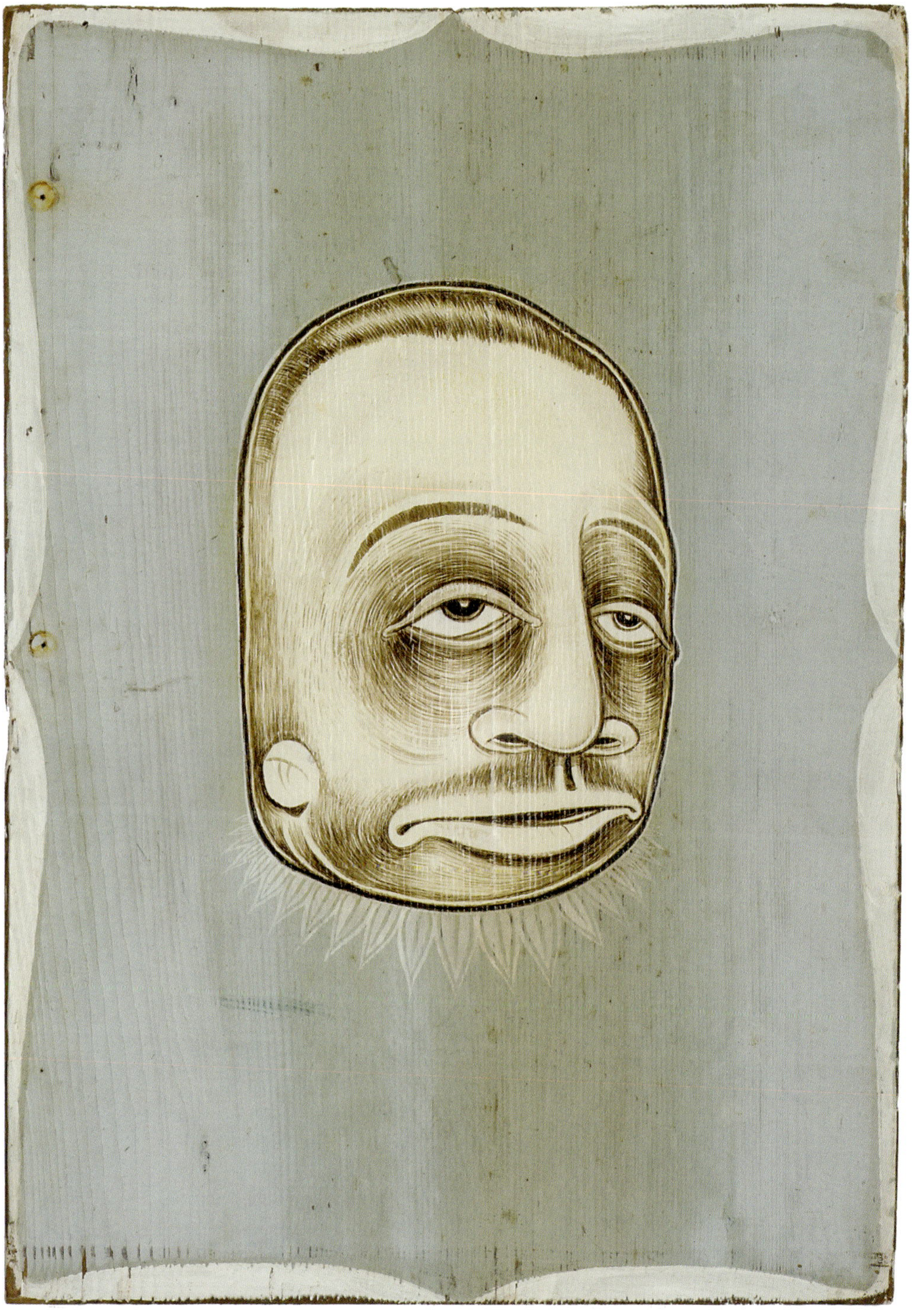

MISSION SCHOOL: YES OR NO?

Excerpts from a panel discussion held on Sunday, October 20, 2013, from 2:00 to 4:00 p.m. in conjunction with ENERGY THAT IS ALL AROUND. *Speakers: Dena Beard, David Kasprzak,* ***Kevin Killian****, Ruby Neri, and* ***Renny Pritikin****.*

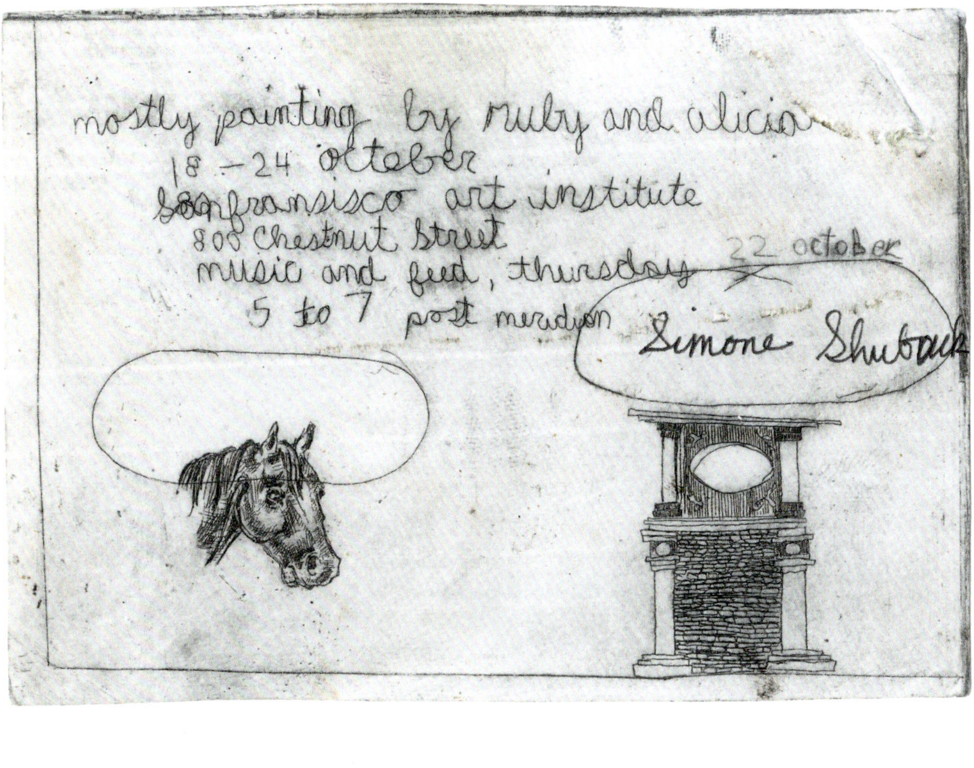

Exhibition postcard
MOSTLY PAINTING BY RUBY AND ALICIA, 1993

BY RENNY PRITIKIN

IT'S PROBABLY AN APOCRYPHAL NOTION that we've all heard all our lives about Eskimos and their dozens of words for snow. The conclusion to draw of course is that we pay very close attention to that which both surrounds us and matters in some significant way to us. I know Yiddish has lots of words for penis (*putz, schmuck, shlong*) that all have the not so much feminist but anti-male connotation of stupidity and pathos, extending from the part to the whole man. English seems to abound in words about how people set themselves apart from each other in small social groups. What that says about us we'll leave for another conversation. Here's a smattering of such words with definitions from my *Webster's* 3rd, 1971, dictionary:

A *clique*, *circle*, and *coterie* are all defined almost identically, as a group with common interests. Coterie gets the added element of intimacy. All three imply that the groupness is at least partially seen from the outside.

BY KEVIN KILLIAN

IN JULY Renny Pritikin invited me to join this panel and to speak to the question of schools from a "literary point of view." As he put it, "Is there a helpful meaning attached to the Beats, the New York School, the Language poets, etc., in terms of understanding history, getting insight into regionalism, defining community, whatever." So I've had a while to think about it, and I've thought of these things continually over the past year, and I'll tell you why.

I came to San Francisco from New York in 1980, and three things struck me right away—one of them was that cars don't honk here, another one was that the city was packed with artists whose names I had literally never heard before, and three, that it was the perfect place for me. Unwittingly I had moved to the very neighborhood where a writing avant-garde was in formation, and I became a recruit. . . .

I was thinking of the Mission School in terms of the Western, well, in a way you can't help it, for its range of

A *faction* is a clique that is often contentious, self-seeking, or reckless of the common good. Of course this has nothing to do with the Mission School.

More interesting are the following two words: A *set* is a number of persons associated by custom, occupation, social activity, or age. A *school* is a group of artists under a common local or personal influence producing a general similarity in their work, or the art of a region. (I would add the metaphor of a school of fish, moving together to foil common enemies.)

By the fact that these five artists are the same age and lived in the same neighborhood at the same time and shared many of the same values and interests, they fit the dictionary definition. In a review of the show I wrote that "they chose to paint or draw on cheap, faded, stained, and torn commercial paper, or pieces of quarter-inch plywood or doorskin found discarded in the street or at construction sites, or on walls, fences, and freight trains. Secondly, their figuration pays homage to all sorts of Western arcana, from Frederic Remington to Indian signs, from railroad and saloon advertising to the painting of the pueblo. Its ethic is a call to a time before law, a utopian vision of a particular moment in history, even before economy, as evidenced by the extra-juridical aspects of tagging, of graffiti, of making a work to exist outside of the market, actually flouting the market as it were by creative work for literal "public consumption." But in the formation of writing groups (and I know little about how art groups are born and made), there is a sociological sense that the in-group and out-group are signs of what social psychologists call coalition affiliation. Such affiliation is not necessarily a sign of kinship. . . . Indeed one could say this whole panel we sit on today is anxiety-driven, or at least the question we were given, Mission School—yes or no? This is hard for Californians to answer, we're more like, *Well, on the one hand this, but on* drawing styles were improvised, fugitive, rejecting of the abilities of a traditional skilled hand, and rather, soaked in arcane social histories, whether of surfing, skating, hoboing, or folk music, typography, and design. When figurative, the work was influenced by comix and a reflection of the grittiest parts of urban life lived in post-student poverty."

Other notions we might think about is how artists in a school learn from and compete and influence each other. Also not mentioned in the dictionary are four more effects of a school: (1) their impact on succeeding generations, as in "gonna skool ya," (2) media promotion (getting taken up by mass media, note Jerry Saltz on Facebook this week complaining about the request for interviews he's gotten from mainstream media about Banksy in New York), (3) the art industry's attention (in the case of Mission School, New Yorkers Annie Philbin of the Drawing Center and Jeffrey Deitch, the commercial dealer), and (4) the artist's style and charisma.

the other hand that. Yes or no? We don't need that sort of pressure, we're in a both/and sort of place—at least we are in theory. . . .

Nearly twenty years ago I wrote a review for *Artweek* asking about a show at Paule Anglim I had attended. It was one of their *Sight/Vision* shows, curated by Bill Berkson, featuring Wallace Berman, Jay DeFeo, Wally Hedrick, George Herms, Bruce Conner, and Jess. I wrote in, I love all these artists, but why are you grouping them together over and over again? It is making an iron enclosure out of what was actually a very fluid scene. This was the 1995 edition of this show, and oddly enough, or so I thought, the list of artists exactly replicated those covered by Rebecca Solnit in her wonderful book *Secret Exhibition: Six California Artists of the Cold War Era.* Come on, add someone different! The result of such formations, I argued, was to shut out other worthy artists, so my argument

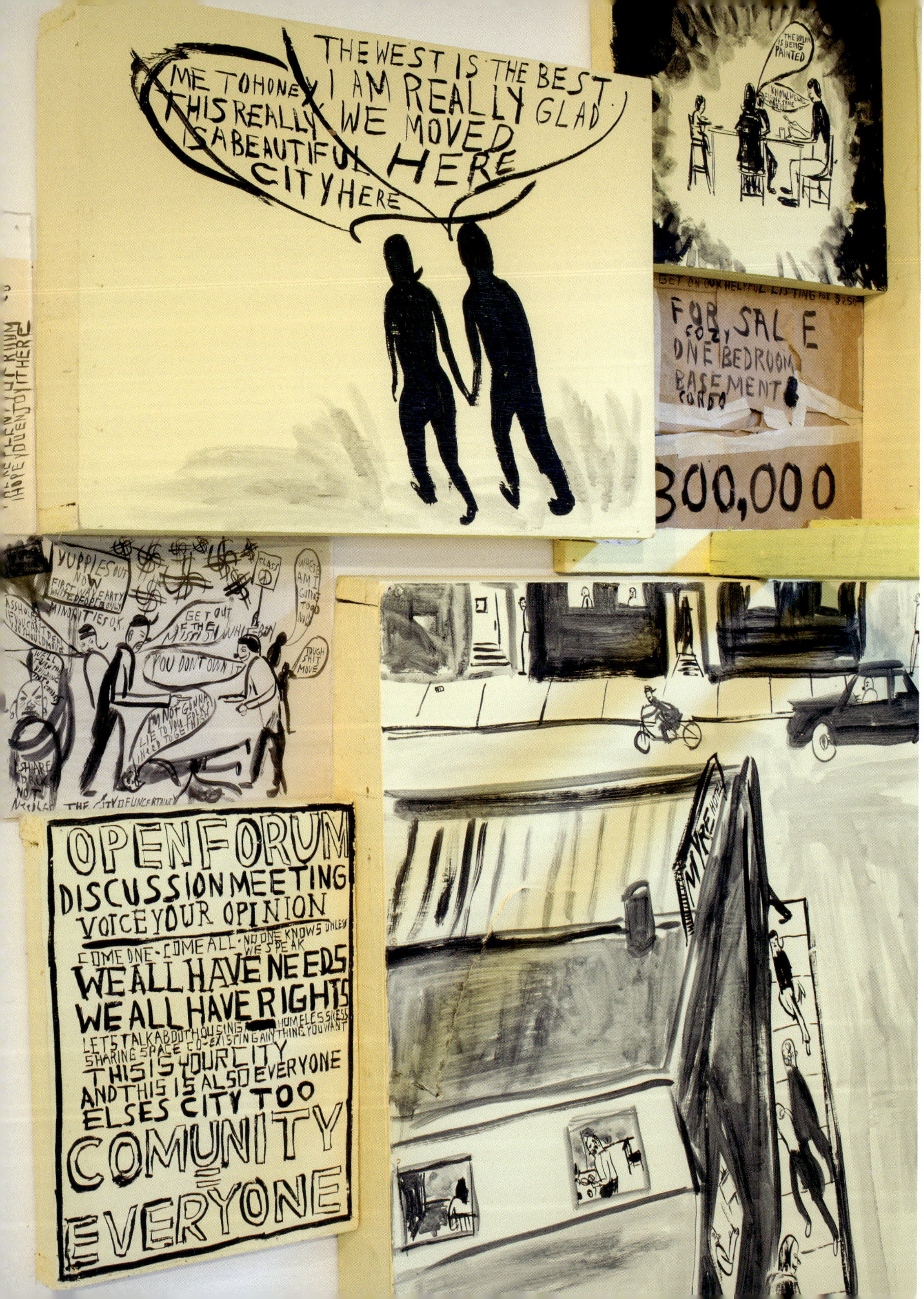
THE WEST IS THE BEST
I AM REALLY GLAD WE MOVED HERE
ME TOHONEY THIS REALLY IS A BEAUTIFUL CITY HERE
THE ROOM IS BEING PAINTED
FOR SALE
COZY
ONE BEDROOM
BASEMENT
CONDO
300,000
YUPPIES OUT NOW
YOU DONT OWN IT
TOUGH SHIT MOVE
OPEN FORUM
DISCUSSION MEETING
VOICE YOUR OPINION
COME ONE · COME ALL · NO ONE KNOWS UNLESS WE SPEAK
WE ALL HAVE NEEDS
WE ALL HAVE RIGHTS
THIS IS YOUR CITY
AND THIS IS ALSO EVERYONE
ELSES CITY TOO
COMUNITY
=
EVERYONE

Perhaps some of these factors elucidate why the Beat poets became an internationally promoted school, but twenty years later San Francisco's Language poets, arguably at least equally important as poets, are known only in poetry and academic circles. The hippie bands of the '60s—Grateful Dead, Jefferson Airplane, Janis Joplin and Big Brother and the Holding Company—became internationally acclaimed, but not the Center for Contemporary Music at Mills, for example. The Beat artists—DeFeo, Connor, et al.—are increasingly in the canon, but less so the conceptual generation of the *Space/Time/Sound* show, Kos, Fried, Marioni, et al.

I think it is worth noting that chance and personalities play into it as well. The exclusive, coherent nature of a group is based on these things. Chris Johanson is in the Mission School, but a very similar, talented artist of the same generation like Jason Jägel is not. Alicia McCarthy is, but a contemporary like Rebeca Bollinger is not. Terry Hoff

bristled with the righteousness of those with a mission. Of course I had a particular artist in mind—I say, "of course," because is it likely that anyone would complain about such a well-organized group of artists except one representing the refusees? (Here I was thinking of the San Francisco collagist and painter Fran Herndon.)

In fact are all recovery projects, like the one I've mounted on behalf of the late Jack Spicer (1925–1965), manifestations of critical anxiety by nature? Who else but one who fears he or she is in danger of being forgotten himself would project onto others as though fame and appreciation were a human right like the right to water, to rent control, to travel? What makes a group? Is it a shared purpose? Is it a boys' club of shared activity like pounding down beers at the Cedar Tavern? Is there a common opposition to the status quo? Is it an accident of media, like the *Life* magazine photo in which Hedda Sterne was the

left
CHRIS JOHANSON
THE SURVIVALISTS
(installation view), 1999

emerged at the same time, doing very similar work, but lived in Pacifica, and was a little older and straighter, and is not part of the club.

I recently saw for the first time the film made about Philip Guston around the time of his retrospective here at SFMOMA. In it he discusses briefly the New York School. He makes three wonderful points, which round out my thinking about schools:

1. "We electrified each other."

2. The term *New York school* was just geography, no content, so a good name we all could live with.

3. On making art: Start with a roomful of friends, colleagues, critics, then when they leave, you are alone, and then when you leave, someone makes art.

only woman? Do curators, critics, or historians ultimately decide who was in such and such a group and who wasn't? Is this status important only at the moment when money changes hands? You hear people say, "Oh, I was never really a Language poet," but you never hear them say, "Oh, I was never really a U.S. president." It's funny that, since the presidents are the masters of denial in every other aspect of rhetoric, but this one, perhaps because it has a pension attached to it, they affirm their membership in the group with a rare nonpartisan us-ness. So let us do the same; perhaps the pension of history shall follow.

RUBY NERI
UNTITLED (*from* SUCH THING COUNTLESS WONDRS *series*), *1995*

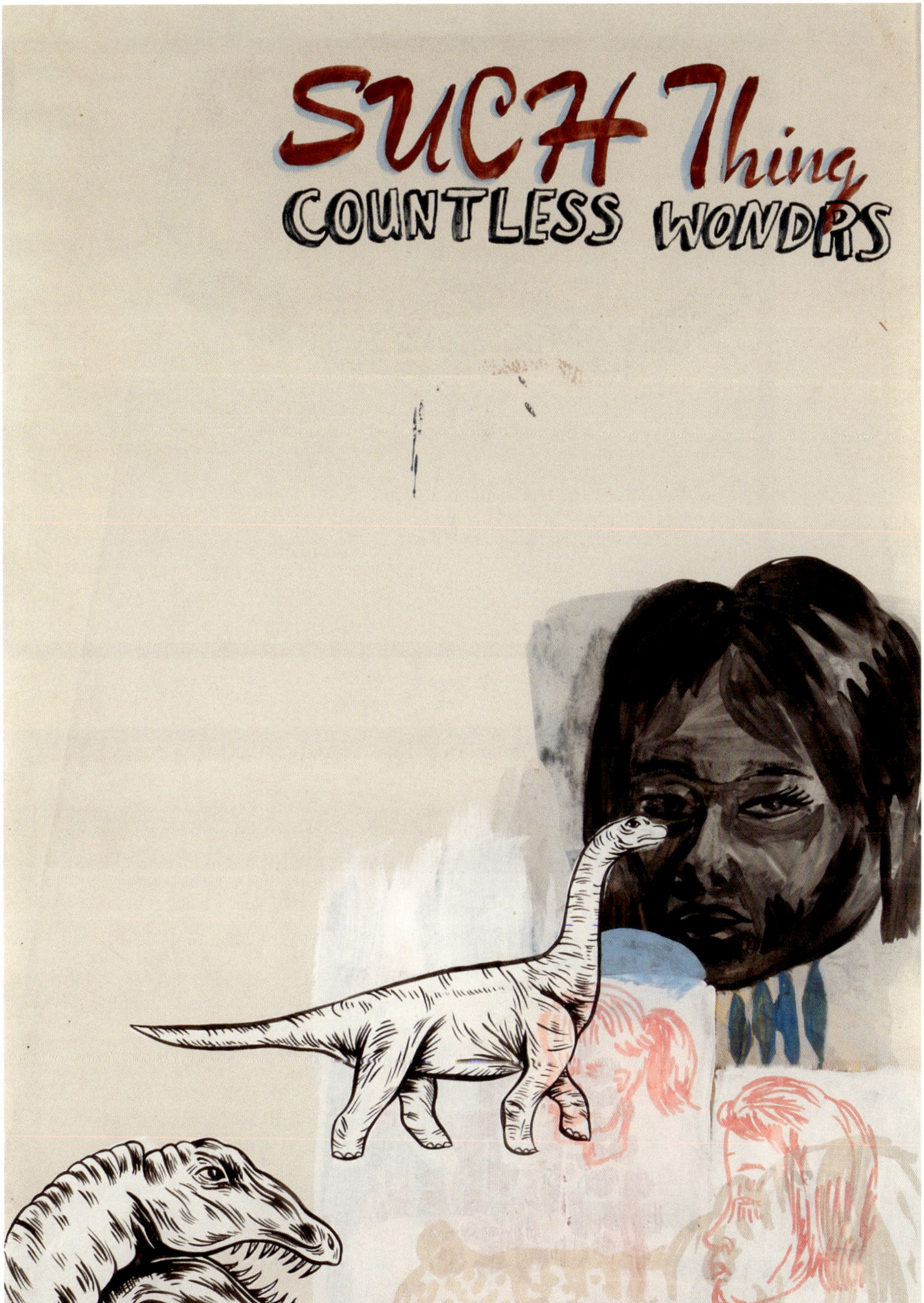
SUCH Thing
COUNTLESS WONDRS

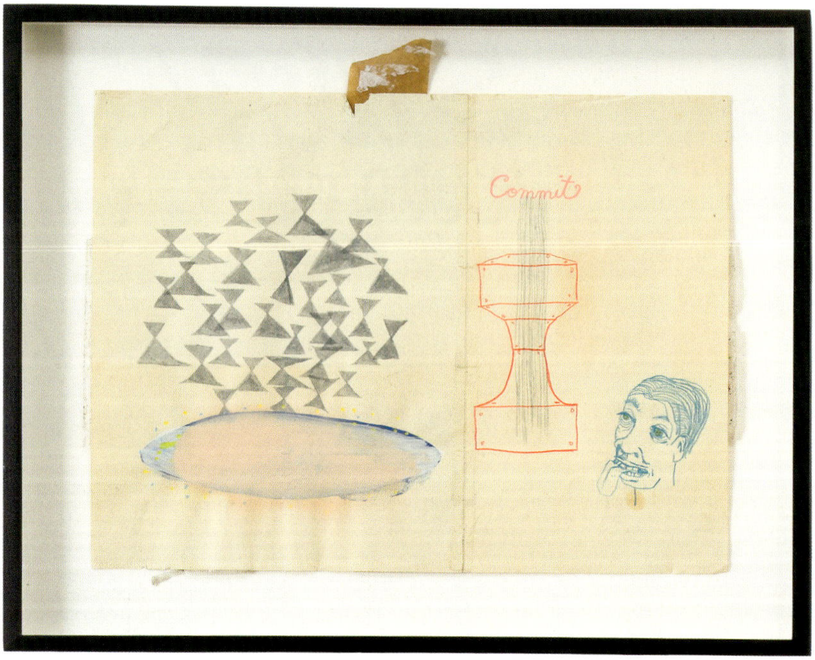
Commit

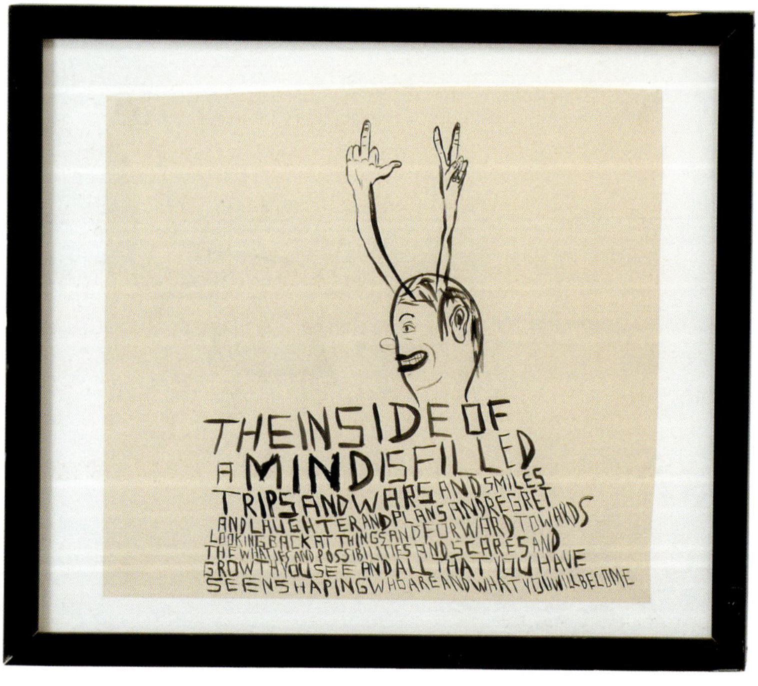
THEINSIDE OF
A MINDISFILLED
TRIPSANDWARS ANDSMILES
ANDLAUGHTERANDPLANSANDREGRET
LOOKINGBACKATTHINGSANDFORWARDTOWARDS
THEWHATIFSANDPOSSIBILITIESANDSCARESAND
GROWTHYOUSEE ANDALLTHATYOUHAVE
SEENSHAPINGWHOAREANDWHATYOUWILLBECOME

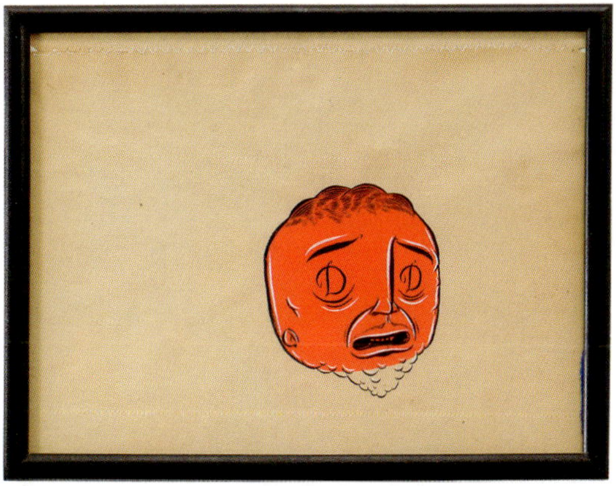

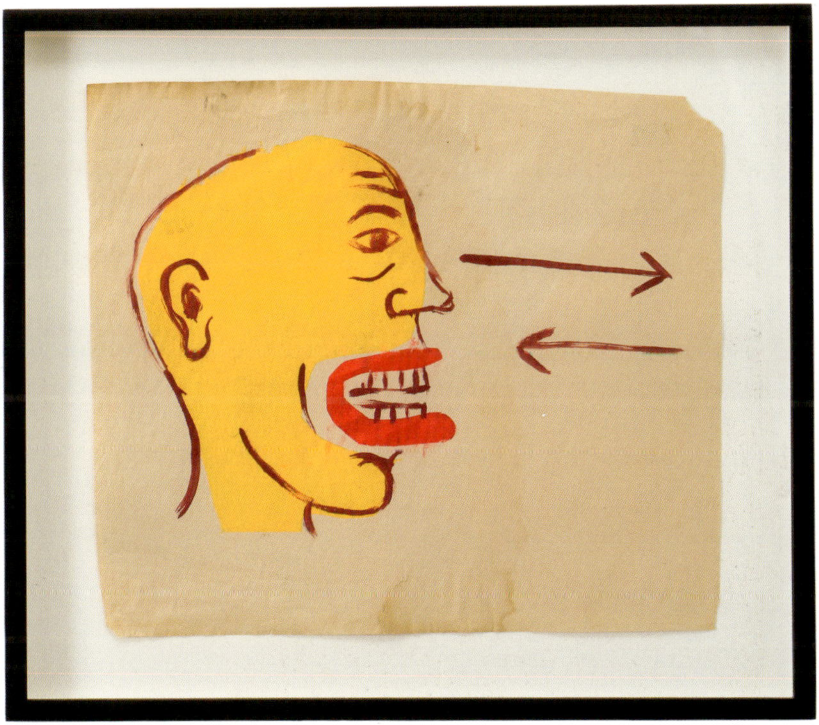

Clockwise from top left:
ALICIA McCARTHY, BARRY McGEE, CHRIS JOHANSON, CHRIS JOHANSON

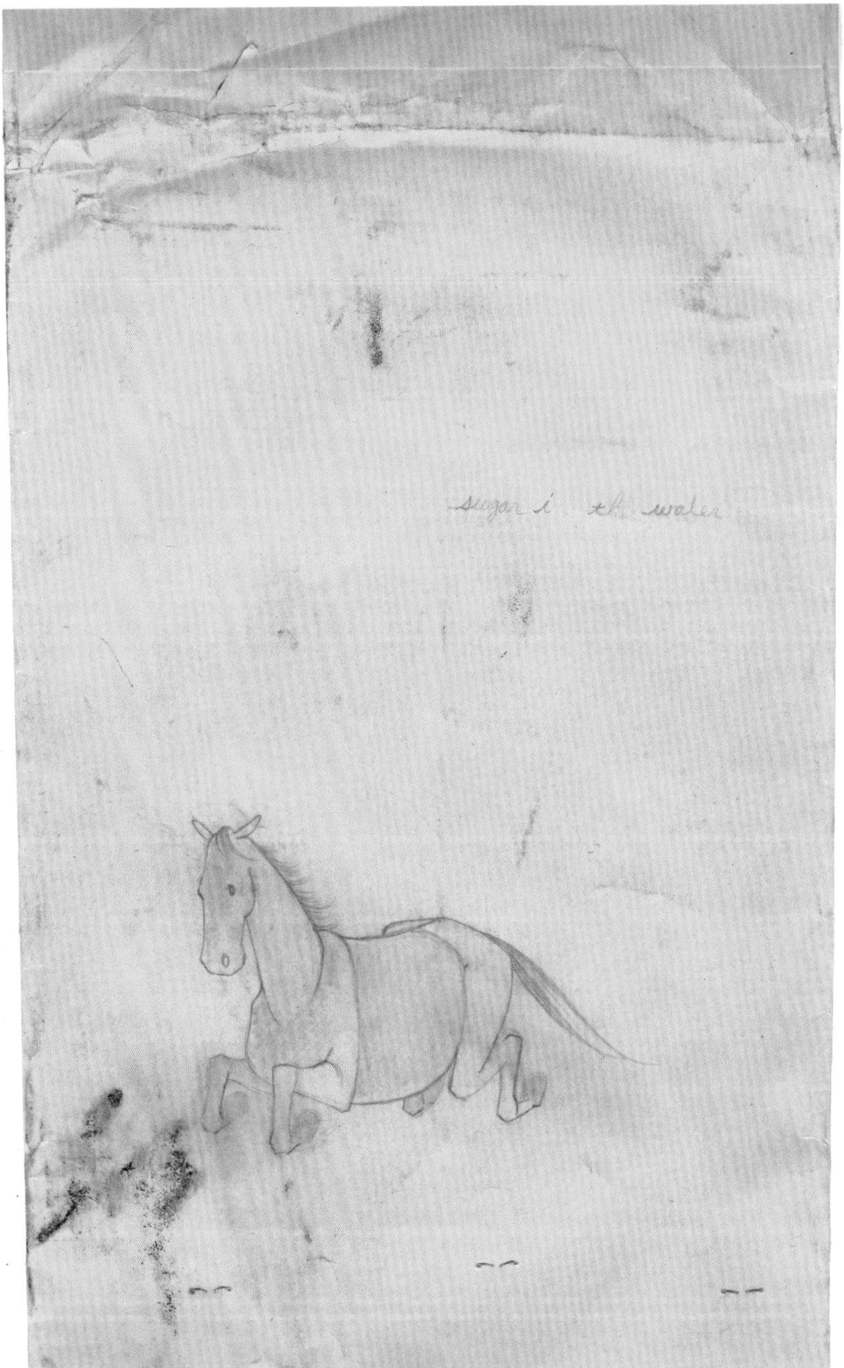
sugar i th water

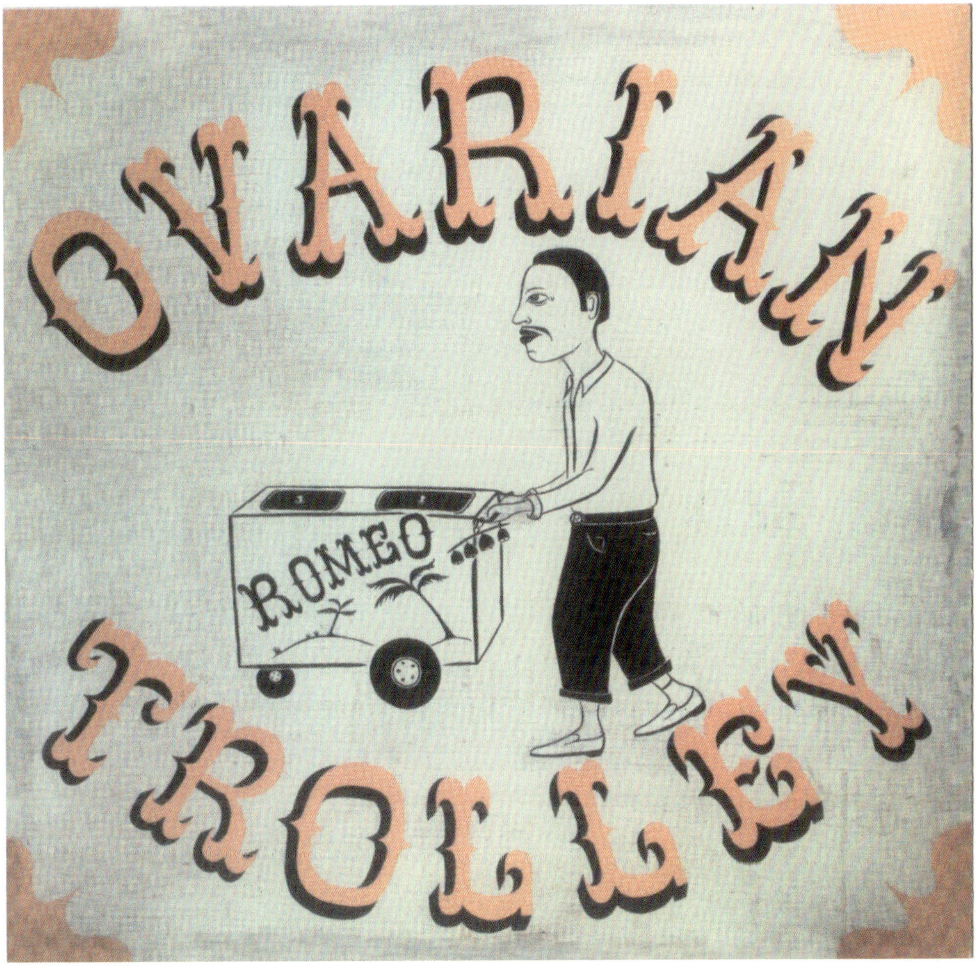

left
RUBY NERI
UNTITLED, *1994*

right
HAZEL/OVARIAN TROLLEY
INCENDIARY/ROMEO, *1997*

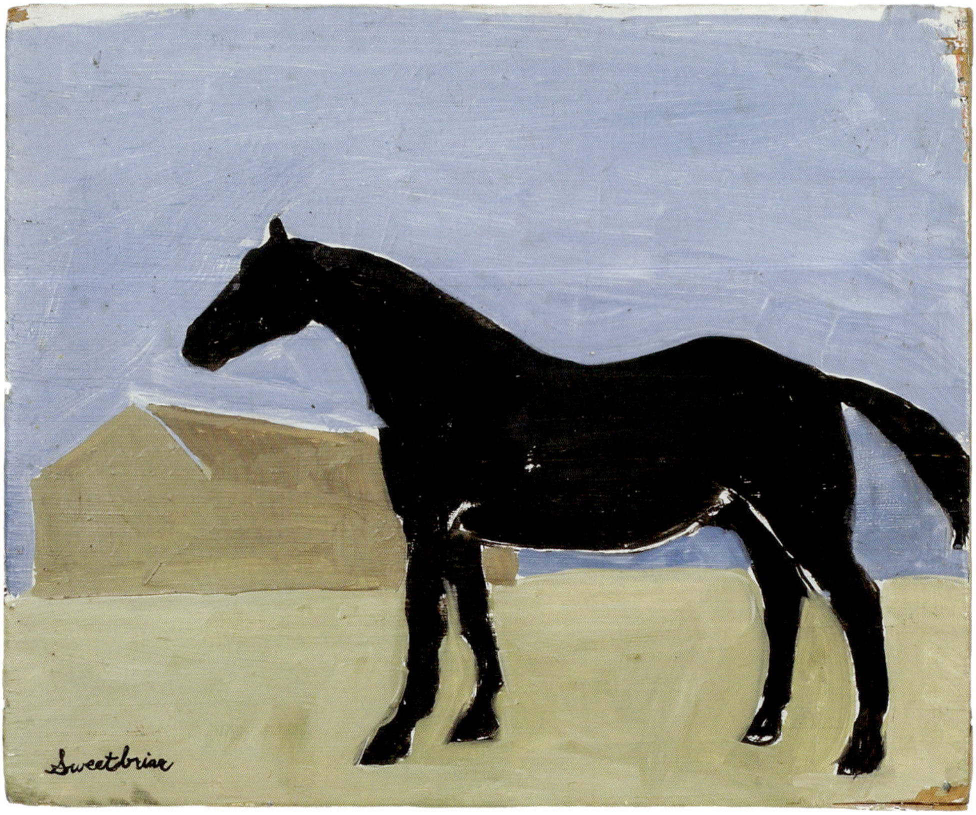
Sweetbriar

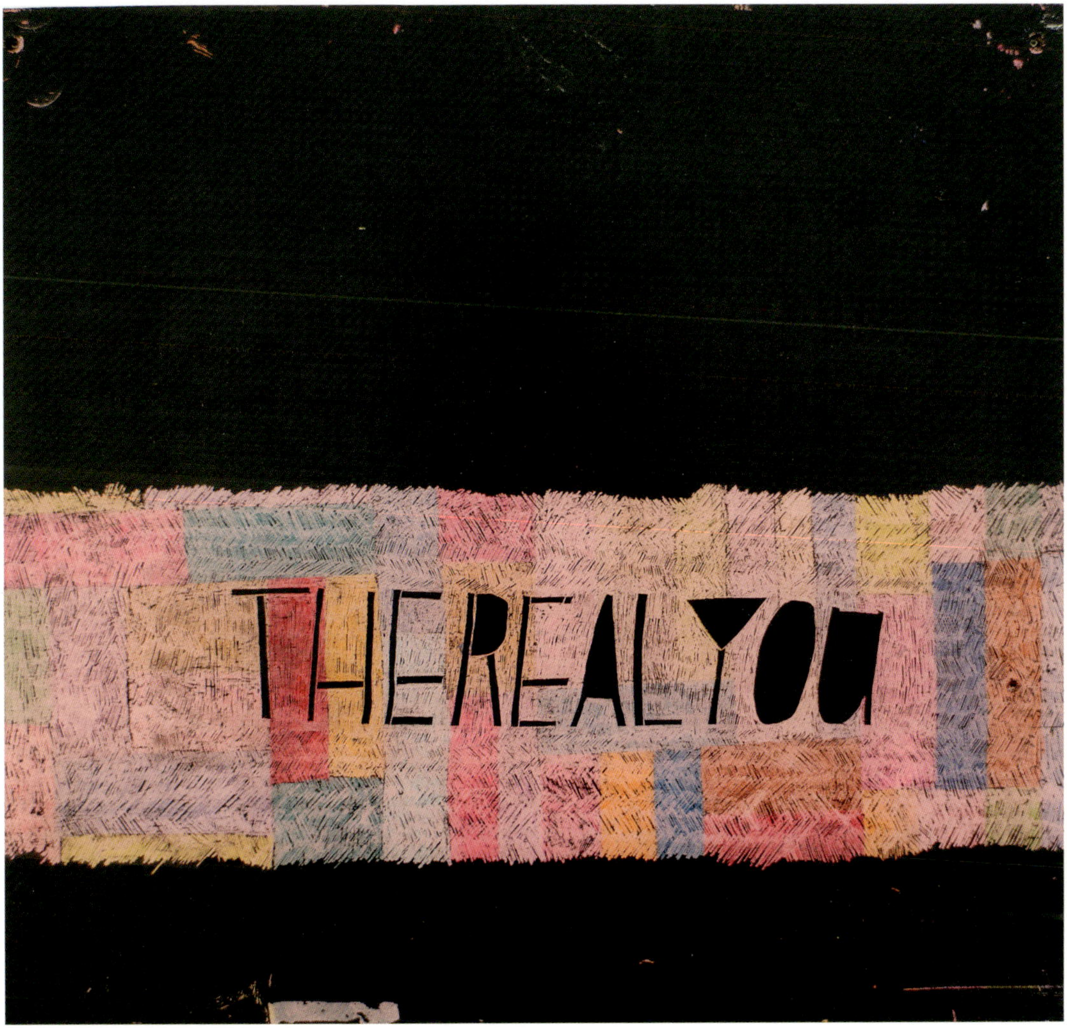

left
RUBY NERI
UNTITLED, *1995*

right
ALICIA McCARTHY
THERE ALL YOU, *2009*

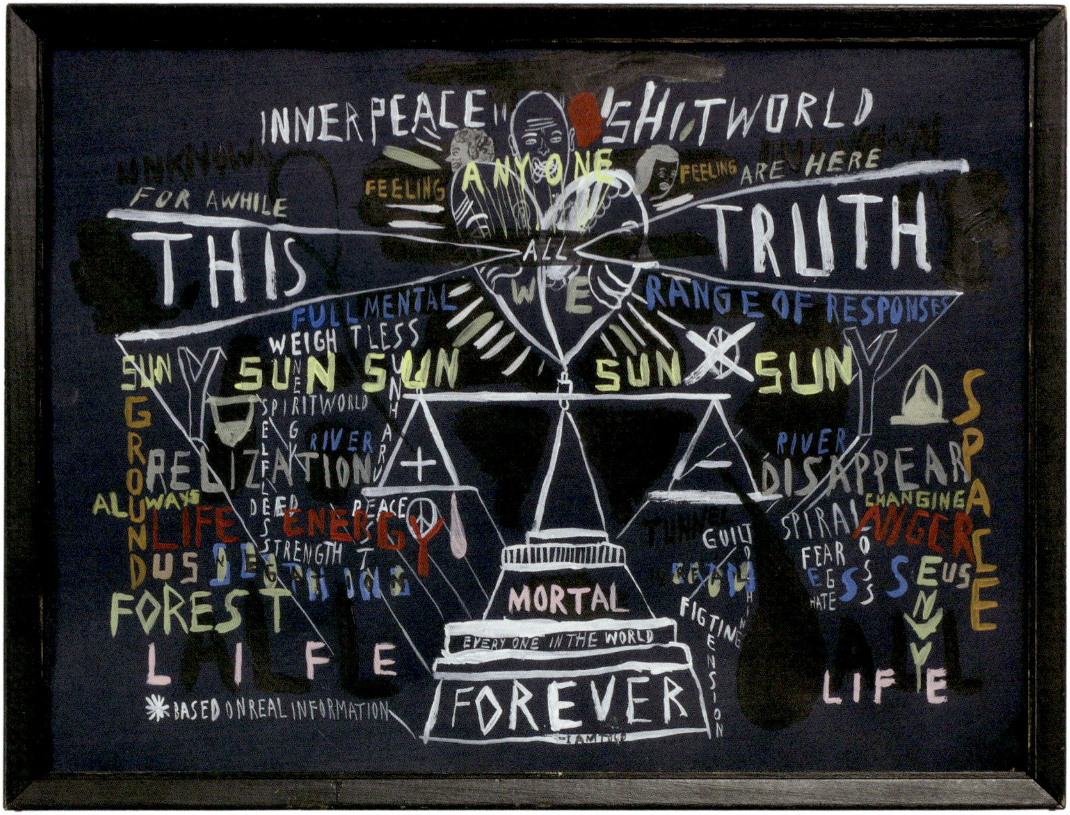
INNERPEACE
SHITWORLD
ANYONE
FEELING
FEELING ARE HERE
FOR AWHILE
THIS
TRUTH
ALL
WE
FULLMENTAL
RANGE OF RESPONSES
WEIGHTLESS
SUN
SUN SUN
SUN
SUN
SPIRITWORLD
RIVER
RIVER
GROUND
RELIZATION
DISAPPEAR
SPACE
ALLWAYS
LIFE
ENERGY
PEACE
STRENGTH
CHANGING
TUNNEL
GUILT
SPIRAL
NIGER
FEAR
HATE
FOREST
MORTAL
EVERY ONE IN THE WORLD
FIGTING
TENSION
LIFE
LIFE
FOREVER
BASED ON REAL INFORMATION

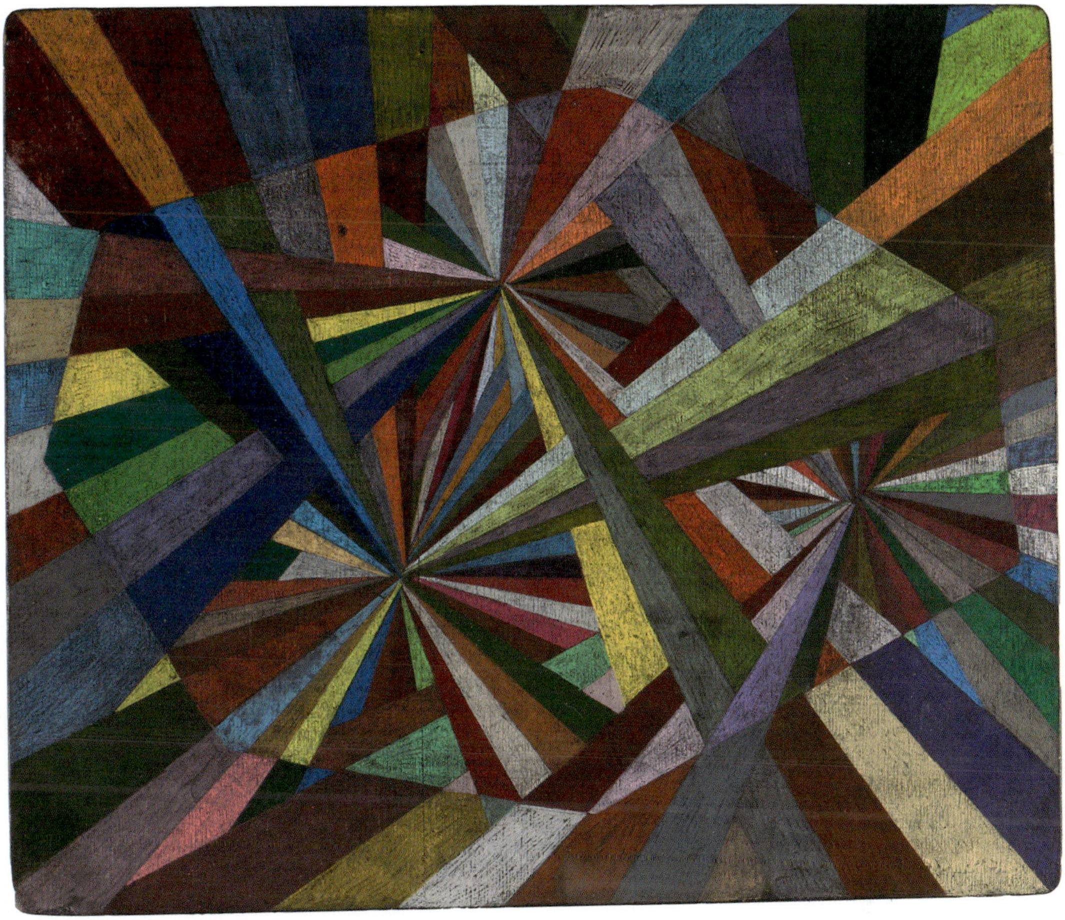

left
CHRIS JOHANSON
WHO REALLY KNOWS
WHAT IS GOING ON, *2000*

right
ALICIA McCARTHY
UNTITLED, *2006*

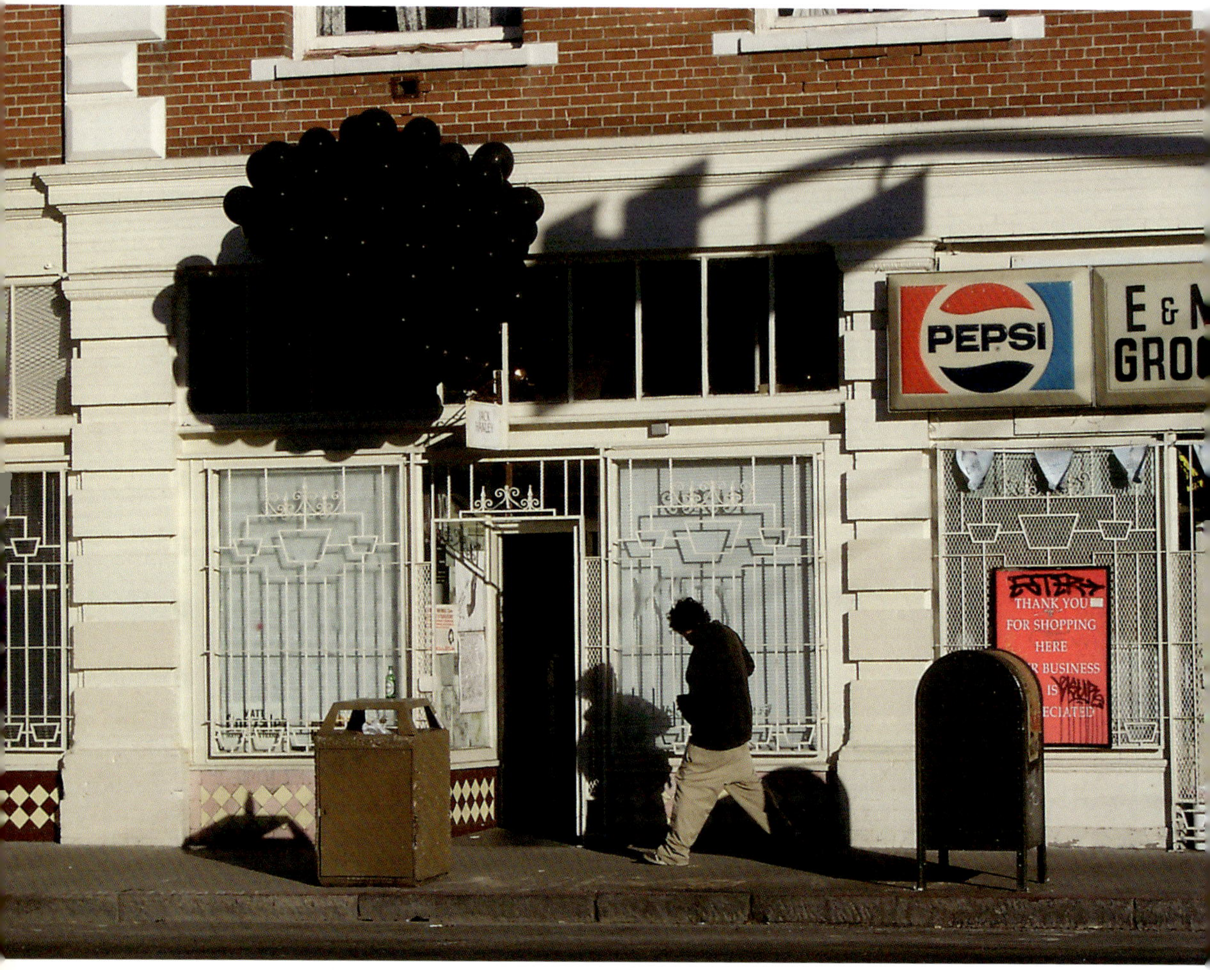
PEPSI
THANK YOU
FOR SHOPPING
HERE

MISSION IN THE RAIN

BY JACK HANLEY

No matter what comes down
the Mission always looks the same

"MISSION IN THE RAIN," WRITTEN BY
JERRY GARCIA AND ROBERT HUNTER

WELL, I'M NOT SURE this is still the case, but at the point that I was showing and interacting with the artists in this show, the Mission did in fact have a day-to-day sameness and regularity that was part of its charm. One of the flatter San Francisco neighborhoods and, because of its geographic location, one of the sunniest, the Mission has always attracted immigrant families, artists, musicians, and other bohemian types for its cheap Mexican food, cafes, and, most important, its cheap rents. The neighborhood seemed to have various hubs, tied to the BART stations at Sixteenth and Twenty-Fourth Street and Mission. The hub at Sixteenth and Valencia was a focal point for me; my gallery was at Fifteenth and Valencia. *Rolling Stone* magazine, years back in the early '90s when these artists were first working there, dubbed the intersection at Sixteenth Street the coolest corner in the United States. Well, certainly there were a lot of used bookstore options (four) and a broad range of international food restaurants serving up excellent inexpensive lunches—Vietnamese, Middle Eastern, pizza, Japanese, French, etc. At night the neighborhood was quite different, with clubs drawing the

17 REASONS *(exterior installation view), 2003*
Jack Hanley Gallery, San Francisco, CA

hipsters from outlying neighborhoods and towns in the Bay Area to the Valencia Street corridor, although a few local bars still functioned as local clubs.

The artists that hung out in my part of the Mission generally frequented Adobe Books and could be found there, or a message could be left there to later meet them in Andrew McKinley's wonderfully open community center/bookstore/gallery/music practice room/poetry reading venue. This hub of activity cross-pollinated the music/art/writing scenes, and the mix and the friendliness was contagious and great—Beat writer/pigeon repair man Swan's sleeping loft, assorted people nodding off on the couches, bands practicing in the basement, unsold pastries from Tartine bakery every evening. The tight community was reflected in the artists' communal work on projects and social commentary and political awareness not often seen in other cities known for having street art. I think the isolation of San Francisco from the more mainstream art scenes in New York, London, and Berlin gave an unselfconscious encouragement to artists' involvement in forming community and supporting local politics/businesses and each other. This involvement is evident in their work both in subject matter and where it would turn up.

One of the artists, Chris Johanson, grew up in San Jose but quickly moved to San Francisco and the Mission District area, finding the artist/museum/skater mix there receptive to his outpourings. I first met Chris through his punk band Tina, Age 13 and the hand-painted sleeves that he brought over to my gallery space. He also did street drawings and flyers for various shows, benefits, and causes around the area. Later I bought a few of Chris's drawings on newsprint from Kiki Gallery. $50. Each.

While most of the artists that are described as part of the Mission School have been grouped by their geographic connection, there are a few other aspects that also overlap. The use of urban problems as subject matter, with street

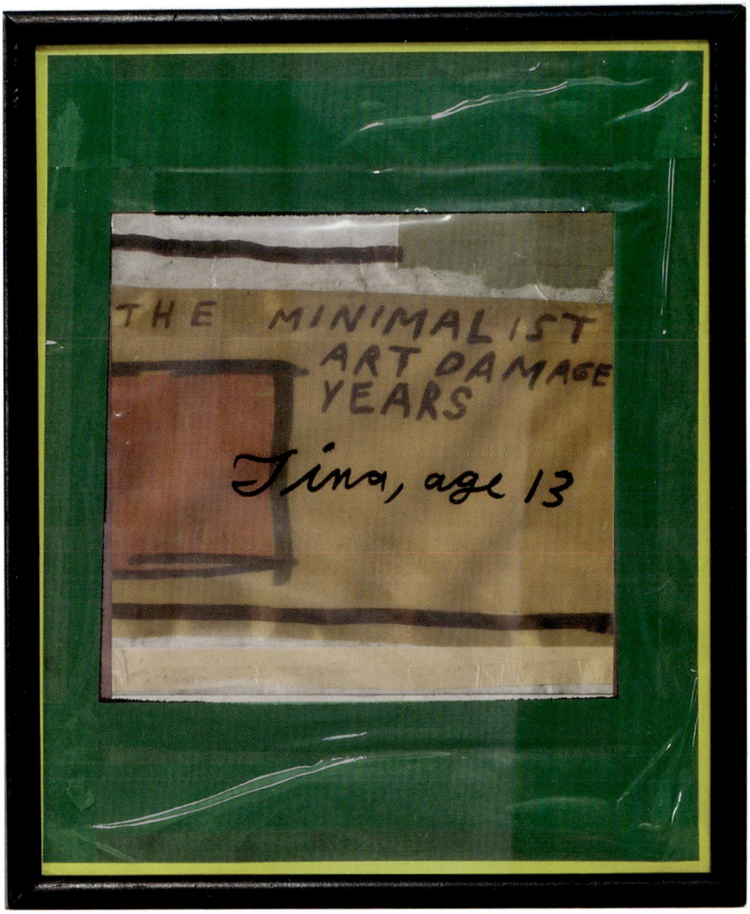

CHRIS JOHANSON
TINA, AGE 13: THE MINIMALIST ART DAMAGE YEARS, *1993*

characters and users, along with the debris of run-down city life (lots of access to scrap wood, found house paint from the recycling center, walls and fences to paint on), revealed content and form of the non–art world and nonacademic variety. This type of street proclamation fit nicely in a neighborhood with a tradition of Mexican mural painting and political posters and tolerance of diversity. Barry McGee and Margaret Kilgallen and Chris Johanson all surfed and skated and graffitied. Alicia McCarthy and Ruby Neri grafittied and also brought it into the studio using found materials. Barry was born in San Francisco and tagged under the name Twist, Ray Fong, Bernon

Vernon, and other names. Depictions of various street people and some reoccurring iconic city types permeated Barry's and Chris's drawings and paintings. The use of found and recycled materials allowed for unusual color combinations using house paint, spray paint, and found bottles/wood/walls/fences/pallets, etc. A sometimes cynical sense of humor and cathartic desperation often strike the viewer simultaneously. Irregularly shaped works were just a few steps from paint on old Shotwell Street buildings/studios. Many of these same artists played in bands at Adobe Books or at my gallery's openings, representing a full range of styles from punk to folk music—Chris Johanson collected a lot of this music in his double CD *Frisco Styles*.

Alicia McCarthy often worked in collaborative packs with friends, whether painting walls, playing music, or installing a show in the gallery. She used text in somewhat poetic, fractured ways and combined these statements on life with recurring motifs of rainbows, colorful rays, or bursts. Typically, Alicia's installation process involved lots of friendly dogs along with human friends and always included some of her friends' work in the show.

Her use of found materials and children's art-class techniques (like painting colors on a board, covering it in black paint, and scratching back into it) were beautifully direct and present. Ruby Neri (also known as Reminisce) worked on outside walls with her horse motif and sometimes with Alicia and others. Clarion Alley, a mural-covered small street in the Mission, had one of these horse pieces for quite a while. This folk quality of street art was even more pronounced in Margaret Kilgallen's (or Meta's) street paintings and gallery installations referencing early American sign painting and typography. Her hand-lettered paintings and works on found paper mashed contemporary interests and concerns with earlier handmade approaches to advertising and imagery.

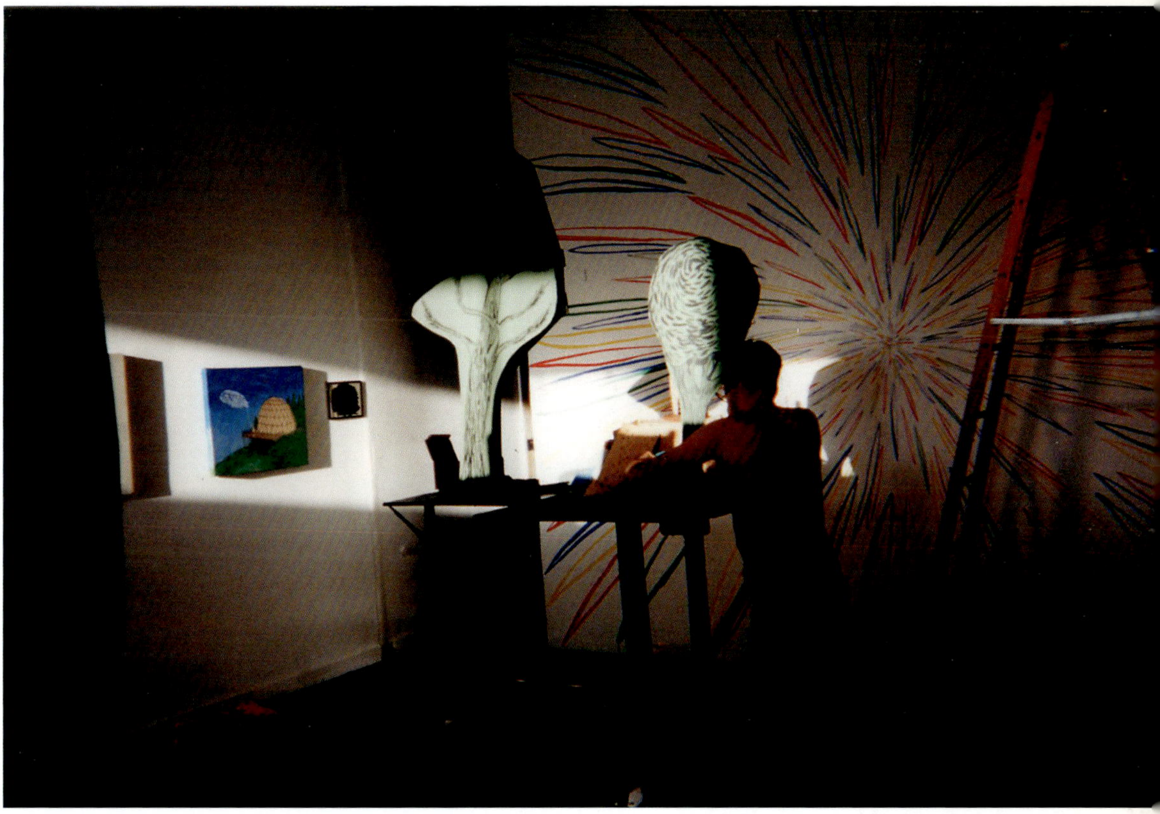

Recycling and using found/free materials in a handmade way was not only economical for artists making little income but also tied in to their philosophical and political ideas, of voting with your dollars, green energy, and supporting local economies and communities. When I first got my space at Valencia and Fifteenth Street, it was between me and a gun shop that the landlord had to choose from. Being next to a liquor store and across the street from Valencia Gardens projects, I think it was good that I got the space, although a gallery was almost as suspect. The artists of the neighborhood sold little and mostly did work for themselves and each other. I think that is probably as it should be.

CHRIS JOHANSON
RELATIONISM ABOUT BROWNNESS *(installation documentation)*, 2001
Jack Hanley Gallery, San Francisco, CA

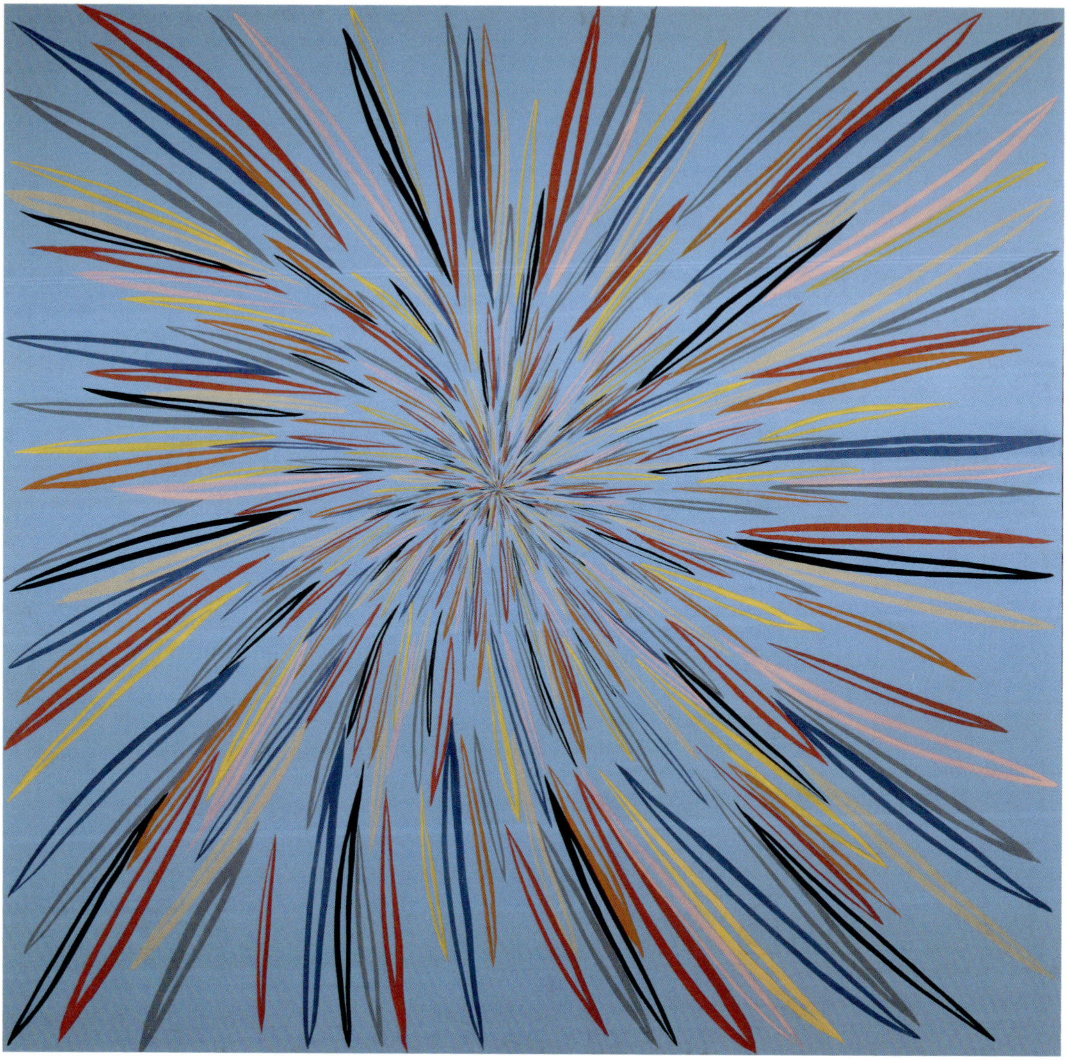

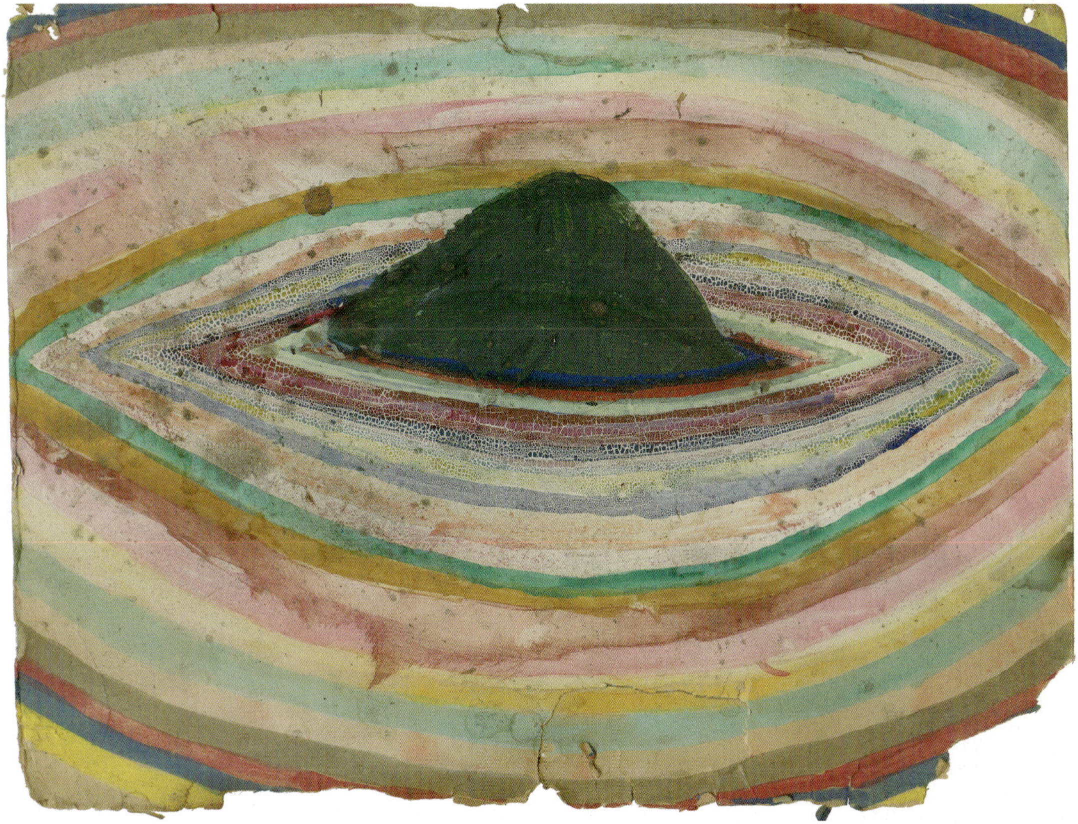

left
CHRIS JOHANSON
THIS CONCEPTUAL ART IS AN ENERGY EXPLOSION ABOUT POSITIVE ENERGY, *2002*

right
ALICIA McCARTHY
UNTITLED, *1994*

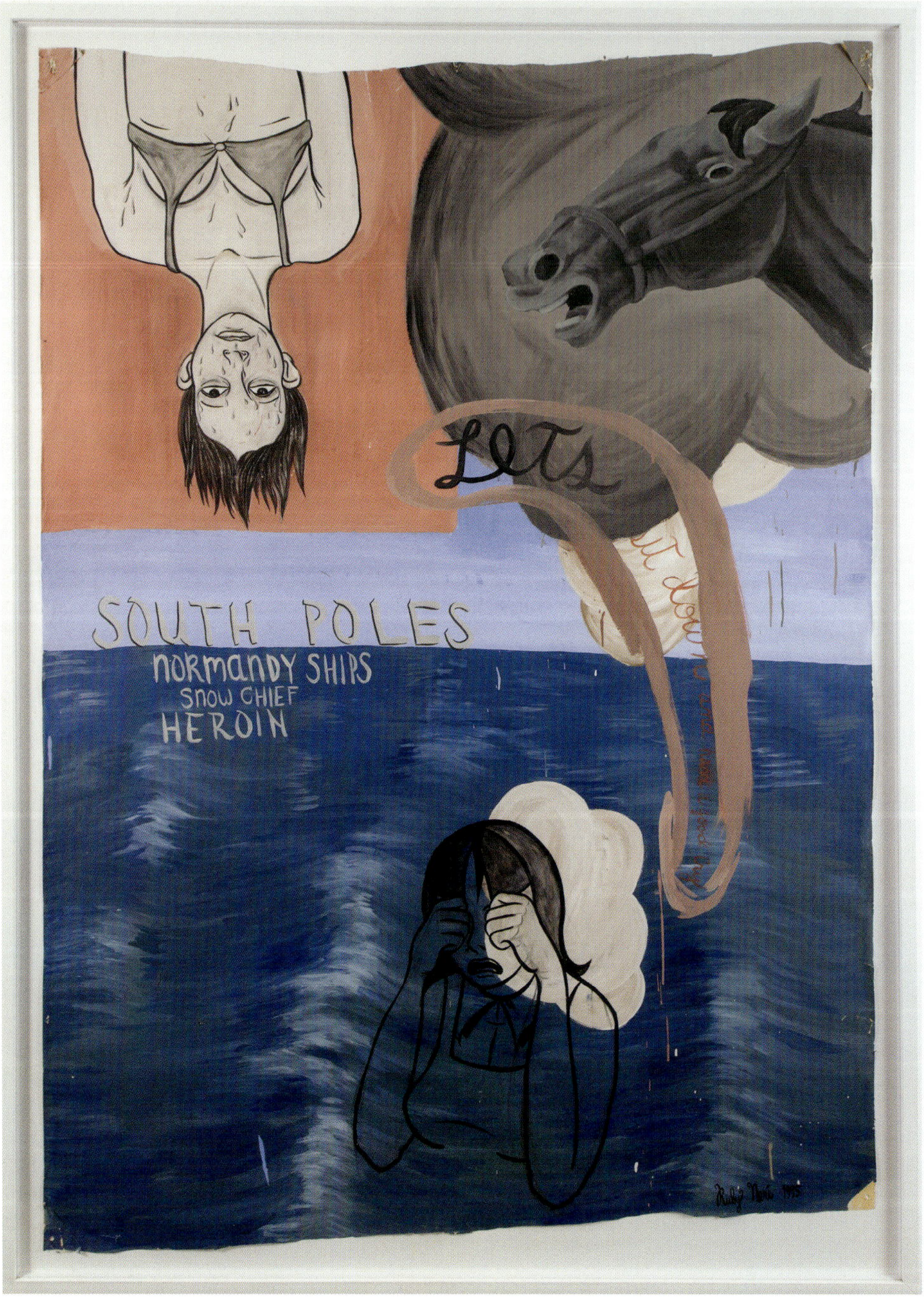

left
RUBY NERI
UNTITLED, *1995*

right
MARGARET KILGALLEN
UNTITLED, *2000*

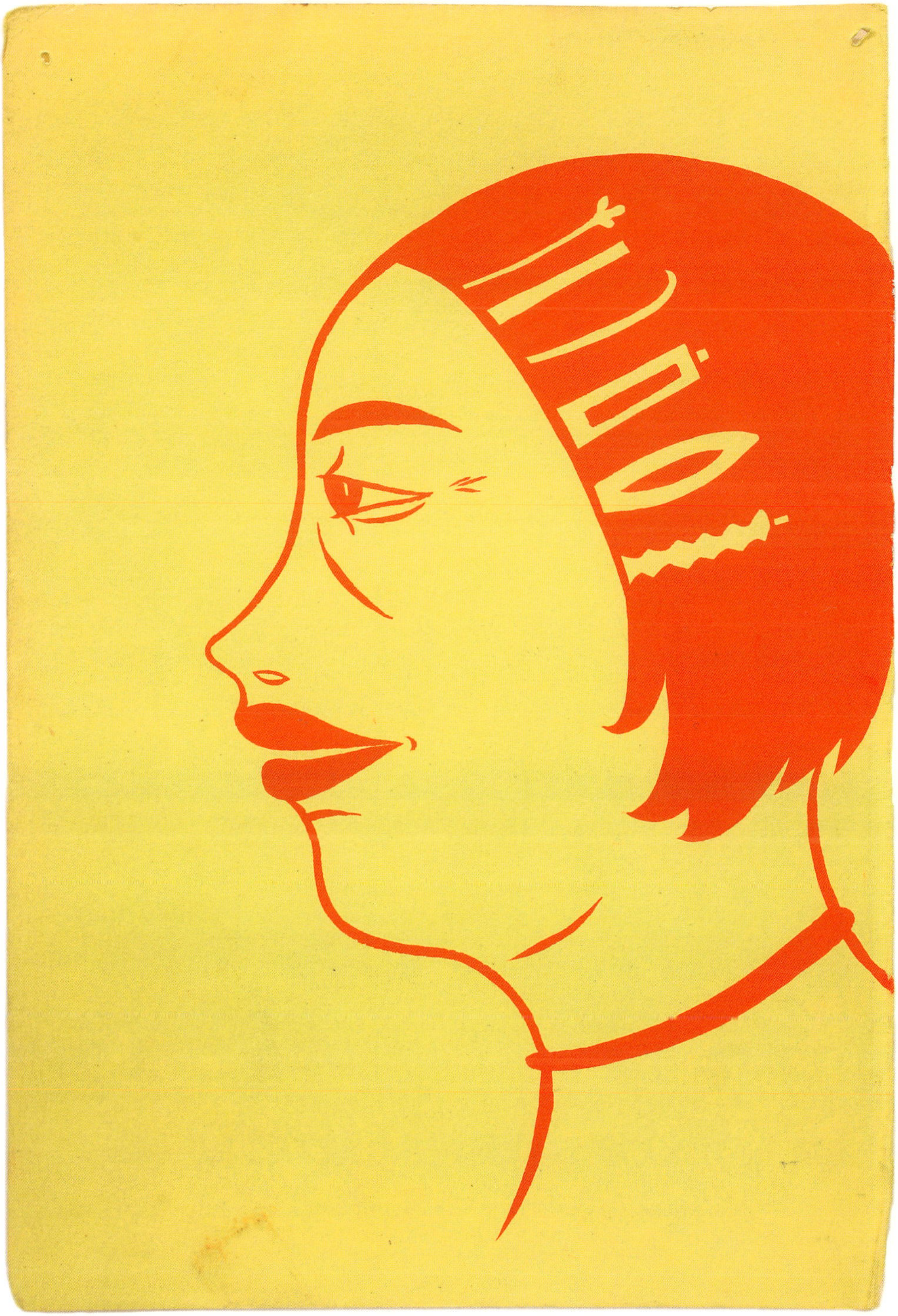

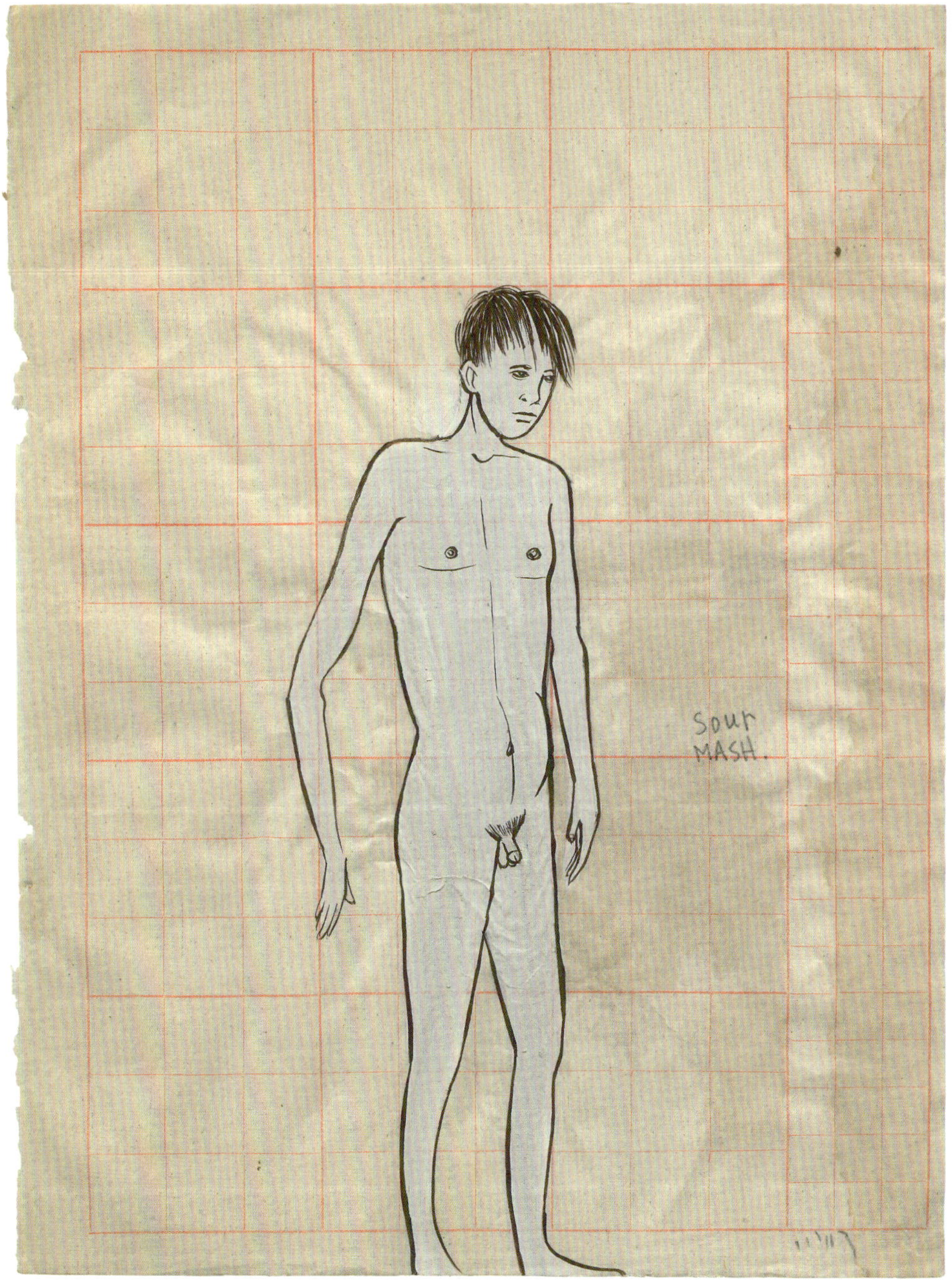
Sour
MASH.

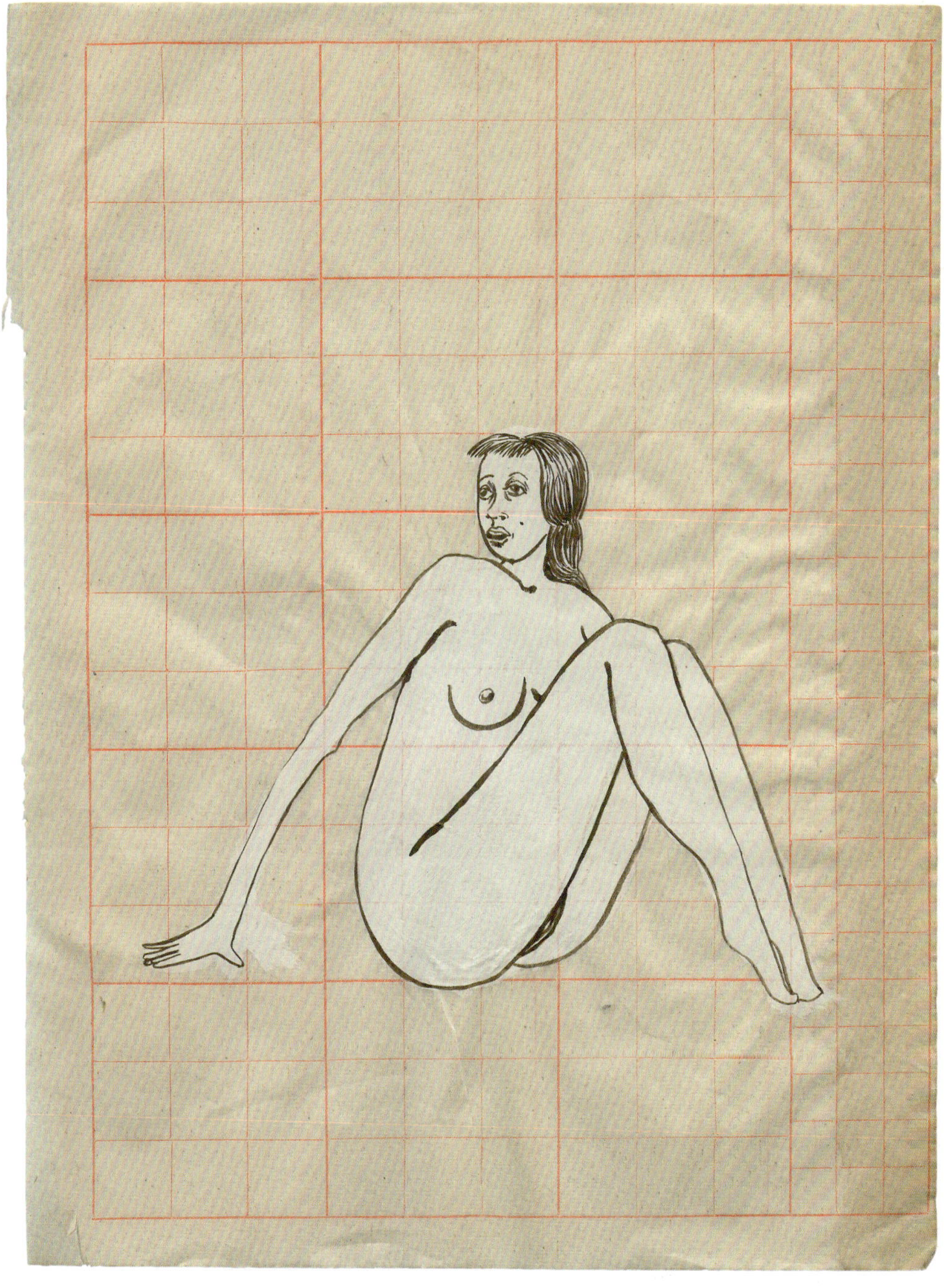

left
RUBY NERI
UNTITLED, *1995*

right
RUBY NERI
UNTITLED, *1995*

ARTIST BIOGRAPHIES

CHRIS JOHANSON

Born in 1968, Chris Johanson currently splits his time between Portland, Oregon, and Los Angeles, California. He was included in the 2002 Whitney Biennial, the 2005 Istanbul Biennial, and the 2006 Berlin Biennial and has exhibited extensively in group and solo shows nationally and internationally, including solo shows at Jack Hanley Gallery and Altman Siegel Gallery in San Francisco; Deitch Projects and Mitchell-Innes & Nash in New York; and Galerie Georg Kargl in Vienna. In 2003, he received a SECA Art Award from SFMOMA. In 2013, Phaidon released a monograph on Johanson as part of its celebrated Contemporary Artists series. Johanson also operates Awesome Vistas, a record label that produces limited-edition vinyl in collaboration with musicians and artists. Johanson is represented by Altman Siegel Gallery, San Francisco, and Mitchell-Innes & Nash, New York.

MARGARET KILGALLEN

Margaret Kilgallen was born in 1967 in Washington, D.C. She received a BA in printmaking from Colorado College in 1989 and an MFA from Stanford University in 2001. Her work has been shown at Deitch Projects and the Drawing Center in New York; Yerba Buena Center for the Arts and the Luggage Store Gallery in San Francisco; and the Institute of Contemporary Art, Boston. Other significant exhibitions include the 2002 Whitney Biennial; the 2005 survey exhibition *Margaret Kilgallen: In the Sweet Bye & Bye* at REDCAT, Los Angeles; and the 2004–6 touring exhibition *Beautiful Losers: Contemporary Art and Street Culture*. Kilgallen passed away prematurely in 2001. Her estate is represented by Ratio 3, San Francisco.

ALICIA McCARTHY

Alicia McCarthy was born in 1969 and lives and works in Oakland, California. She received her BFA from the San Francisco Art Institute in 1994 and also attended the Skowhegan School of Painting and Sculpture and the New York Studio School. In 2007, she received an MFA from the University of California, Berkeley. Her work has been exhibited in venues including Yerba Buena Center for the Arts and the Luggage Store Gallery in San Francisco, and Deitch Projects and RARE Gallery in New York. Honors include an artist residency at the Headlands Center for the Arts and a 2013 Artadia Award. McCarthy is represented by Jack Hanley Gallery, New York.

BARRY McGEE

Born in 1966 in California, Barry McGee received a BFA in painting and printmaking from the San Francisco Art Institute in 1991. Known by the tag name "Twist" for his graffiti and street art, McGee has also developed a career within museums and galleries, exhibiting drawings, paintings, prints, and large-scale, mixed-media installations that take inspiration from urban culture, incorporating elements such as empty liquor bottles, cans of spray paint, signs, scrap wood or metal, surfboards, and other found materials. His work has been shown at the Walker Art Center, Minneapolis; SFMOMA; the Hammer Museum, Los Angeles; Deitch Projects, New York; and the 2001 Venice Biennale. A midcareer survey was recently on view at the Berkeley Art Museum and Pacific Film Archive (BAM/PFA) and the Institute of Contemporary Art, Boston. McGee is represented by Ratio 3, San Francisco, and presented a major exhibition at Cheim & Read, New York, in September 2013.

RUBY NERI

Ruby Neri was born in the 1970s into the collegial environment of artists in San Francisco. Her initial influences were the painters and ceramicists closely associated with her father, the Bay Area Figurative sculptor Manuel Neri. While studying at the San Francisco Art Institute, Neri worked as a street artist under the name "Reminisce," or "REM." Her later influences include American folk artists, early twentieth-century German expressionists, and midcentury modern European sculptors. Neri holds a BFA from SFAI and an MFA from the University of California, Los Angeles. She has had solo exhibitions at David Kordansky Gallery and China Art Objects in Los Angeles and John Natsoulas Gallery in Davis, California, among other venues. Group exhibitions include *Made in LA 2012*, organized by the Hammer Museum and LAXART, and *Bitch Is the New Black*, curated by Emma Gray for Honor Fraser, Los Angeles. Neri is represented by David Kordansky Gallery.

CAPTIONS AND CREDITS

Installation views are of *ENERGY THAT IS ALL AROUND*, Walter and McBean Galleries, San Francisco Art Institute, San Francisco, CA, September 12–December 14, 2013.
All installation photos are by Johnna Arnold/SFAI unless otherwise noted.

COVER
Alicia McCarthy
5 Points Innersecting (detail), 2013
Mural with spray and latex paint;
95 x 461 inches
Courtesy of the artist
Photo credit: Johnna Arnold/SFAI

PAGES 2–3
Opening reception, *ENERGY THAT IS ALL AROUND*, Walter and McBean Galleries, San Francisco Art Institute, San Francisco, CA, September 12–December 14, 2013
Photo credit: Shane O'Neill/SFAI

PAGE 6
Opening reception, *ENERGY THAT IS ALL AROUND*
Photo credit: Shane O'Neill/SFAI

PAGE 9
Barry McGee, Margaret Kilgallen, Alicia McCarthy, and Ruby Neri, 1994
Silver gelatin print
Courtesy of Ruby Neri

PAGE 10
Chris Johanson
The Survivalists (installation view), 1999
Mixed media;
Dimensions variable
Courtesy of the artist

PAGE 13
Margaret Kilgallen
Untitled, ca. 2000
Paint on wood, two elements;
60 x 85 inches overall
Courtesy of the Estate of Margaret Kilgallen and Ratio 3, San Francisco, CA

PAGE 16
Barry McGee
Untitled, 1990–2013
Paint on wood panel;
40 x 90 inches
Courtesy of the artist and Ratio 3, San Francisco, CA

PAGE 17
Barry McGee
Untitled (installation view), ca. 1998
Photographs in artist frame;
14¾ x 50 inches
Courtesy of the artist and Ratio 3, San Francisco, CA

PAGES 20–21
ENERGY THAT IS ALL AROUND (installation view)

PAGE 23
Letter dated April 8, 1992
Addressed to Alicia McCarthy from Michael Grady, dean of students, San Francisco Art Institute
Courtesy of the artist

PAGE 26
Alicia McCarthy notebook page, ca. 1996
Courtesy of the artist

PAGE 29
Margaret Kilgallen
Untitled, 1997
Paint on wood with coins;
29 x 15 x 5 inches
Courtesy of Alexandra Bowes, San Francisco, CA

PAGES 32–43
ENERGY THAT IS ALL AROUND (installation view), Walter and McBean Galleries, San Francisco Art Institute, San Francisco, CA, September 12–December 14, 2013

PAGE 44
Chris Johanson and Johanna Jackson
Untitled (installation view), 2004
Flat paint on wood with video monitors; dimensions variable
Beautiful Losers: Contemporary Art and Street Culture, Yerba Buena Center for the Arts, San Francisco
Courtesy of the artist and Yerba Buena Center for the Arts, San Francisco, CA

PAGE 48
Margaret Kilgallen
Installation view, 1997–98
Soap Factory, Minneapolis, MN

PAGES 52–53
Barry McGee
One More Thing (installation view), 2005
Mixed media; dimensions variable
Deitch Projects, New York, NY
Courtesy of the artist and the Deitch Archive, New York, NY

PAGES 56–57
Alicia McCarthy
The Forgoton Works (installation view), 2003
Mixed media; dimensions variable
Jack Hanley Gallery, San Francisco, CA
Courtesy of the artist and Jack Hanley Gallery, New York, NY

PAGES 62–71
ENERGY THAT IS ALL AROUND (installation view), Walter and McBean Galleries, San Francisco Art Institute, San Francisco, CA, September 12–December 14, 2013

PAGE 72
Ruby Neri
Reminisce graffiti, 1992
Courtesy of the artist

PAGE 74
Margaret Kilgallen, ca. 1998
Photograph courtesy of Barry McGee

PAGE 76
San Francisco, ca. 1998
Photograph courtesy of Barry McGee

PAGE 78
Margaret Kilgallen, ca. 1998
Photograph courtesy of Barry McGee

PAGE 80
Barry McGee
Untitled, 1992
Mixed media on metal panels; 84 x 72 inches
Collection of Renny Pritikin, Oakland, CA

PAGE 81
Alicia McCarthy
Untitled, 1995
Bus shelter intervention
Photograph courtesy of Barry McGee

PAGES 82–83
Ruby Neri
Untitled wall mural, ca. 1994
Photograph courtesy of the artist

PAGE 84
Margaret Kilgallen
Surfer Girl, ca. 1992
Acrylic on wood; 14 x 15½ x 1¾ inches
Courtesy of Mariallidia Marcotulli, Bolinas, CA, and the Estate of Margaret Kilgallen and Ratio 3, San Francisco, CA

PAGE 85
Barry McGee
Untitled, 1994
Mixed media on driftwood; 16 x 22 inches
Courtesy of Mariallidia Marcotulli, Bolinas, CA, and the Estate of Margaret Kilgallen and Ratio 3, San Francisco, CA

PAGE 86
Exhibition postcard, *Mostly Painting by Ruby and Alicia*, Diego Rivera Gallery, San Francisco Art Institute, San Francisco, CA, 1993

PAGE 90
Chris Johanson
The Survivalists (installation view), 1999
Courtesy of the artist

PAGE 93
Ruby Neri
Untitled (from *Such Thing Countless Wondrs* series), 1995
Recycled house paint, acrylic paint, marker, collage, and ink on paper; 30 x 20 inches
Courtesy of the artist

PAGES 94–95
Clockwise from top left:

Alicia McCarthy
Untitled, 1992
Etching and mixed media on paper; 15 x 18½ inches
Collection of Ruby Neri, Los Angeles, CA

Barry McGee
Untitled, 2001
Paint on paper; 9¼ x 11¾ inches
Collection of Nancy and Joachim Bechtle, San Francisco, CA

Chris Johanson
The Inside of a Mind, ca. early 1990s
Acrylic on paper; 15 x 17 inches
Collection of Mariallidia Marcotulli, Bolinas, CA

Chris Johanson
Untitled, 1993
Silkscreen on paper, 10 x 12 inches
Courtesy of the artist

PAGE 96
Ruby Neri
Untitled, 1994
Pencil on envelope; 17½ x 9½ inches
Courtesy of the artist

PAGE 97
Hazel/Ovarian Trolley
Incendiary/Romeo, 1997
7-inch vinyl record
Courtesy of Jack Hanley, New York, NY

PAGE 98
Ruby Neri
Untitled, 1994
Pencil on envelope; 17½ x 9½ inches
Courtesy of the artist

PAGE 99
Alicia McCarthy
There All You, 2009
Crayon, latex paint, gouache on found wood; 15¼ x 16½ inches
Courtesy of Jack Hanley Gallery, New York, NY

PAGE 100
Chris Johanson
Who Really Knows What Is Going On, 2000
Acrylic on board with artist's frame; 12¾ x 16¾ inches
Collection of Jack and Connie Tilton, New York, NY
Courtesy of the artist

PAGE 101
Alicia McCarthy
Untitled, 2006
Colored pencil on wood panel; 10 x 12 inches
Courtesy of Jeff Morris, Oakland, CA

PAGE 102
17 Reasons (exterior installation view), 2003
Jack Hanley Gallery, San Francisco, CA
Courtesy Jack Hanley, New York, NY

PAGE 105
Chris Johanson
Tina, Age 13: The Minimalist Art Damage Years, 1993
Cover art, 7-inch vinyl record

PAGE 107
Chris Johanson
Relationism About Brownness (installation documentation), 2001
Jack Hanley Gallery, San Francisco, CA
Courtesy of Jack Hanley, New York, NY

PAGE 108
Chris Johanson
This Conceptual Art Is An Energy Explosion About Positive Energy, 2002
Acrylic on birch panel; 60 x 60 inches
Courtesy of Tom Peters, Los Angeles, CA, and Roberts & Tilton, Culver City, CA

PAGE 109
Alicia McCarthy
Untitled, 1994
Gouache on paper, baked; 11 x 18⅓ inches
Courtesy of the artist

PAGE 110
Ruby Neri
Untitled, 1995
Mixed media on paper; 82 x 58½ inches
Courtesy of Darryl Smith and Laurie Lazar, Luggage Store Gallery, San Francisco, CA

PAGE 111
Margaret Kilgallen
Untitled, 2000
Acrylic on paper; 8¼ x 5½ inches
Courtesy of the Estate of Margaret Kilgallen and Ratio 3, San Francisco, CA

PAGE 112
Ruby Neri
Untitled, 1995
Mixed media on paper; 10¾ x 7½ inches
Courtesy of the artist

PAGE 113
Ruby Neri
Untitled, 1995
Mixed media on paper, 10¾ x 7½ inches
Courtesy of the artist

ENERGY THAT IS ALL AROUND is made possible by the generosity of donors and sponsors.

SFAI thanks the artists, their galleries, and the private lenders for their generosity in lending original works, photographs, and ephemera to this exhibition.

SFAI'S EXHIBITIONS AND PUBLIC PROGRAMS provide direct access to artists and ideas that advance our culture. The Walter and McBean Galleries, established in 1969, present exhibitions at the forefront of contemporary art practice. The gallery serves as a laboratory for innovative and adventurous projects and commissions new work from emerging and established artists. SFAI's Public Programs develop meaningful interactions between artists, students, and audiences through lectures, education opportunities, and artist-driven experiences. Together, the exhibitions and public programs of the San Francisco Art Institute promote an environment that catalyzes the creative processes of its student artists and thinkers, and creates intimate connections between the SFAI community and the public.

Major support for SFAI's Exhibitions and Public Programs is provided by Grants for the Arts/San Francisco Hotel Tax Fund.

Program support is provided by the Harker Fund of the San Francisco Foundation and The Andy Warhol Foundation for the Visual Arts. The Distinguished Visiting Fellowship for Interdisciplinary Painting Practices is funded by the Winifred Johnson Clive Foundation. Ongoing support is provided by the McBean Distinguished Lecture and Residency Fund, the Buck Fund, and the Visiting Artists Fund of the SFAI Endowment.